For the
General Theological Seminary
with the kind regard of
Charles Lewis Slattery

January 1909

CERTAIN AMERICAN FACES

From a photograph by his friend, Dr. S. J. Mixter.

PHILLIPS BROOKS IN HIS STUDY.

CERTAIN
AMERICAN FACES

Sketches from Life

BY

CHARLES LEWIS SLATTERY

NEW YORK
E. P. DUTTON & COMPANY
681 FIFTH AVENUE

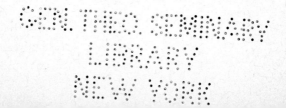

Copyright, 1918
By E. P. DUTTON & COMPANY

Ja 31 '19

Printed in the United States of America

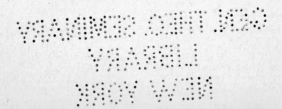

PREFACE

I N England there have been many collec-
tions of short sketches of notable characters in the intellectual and spiritual
realm, all the way from the great classic,
Walton's *Lives,* to Mr. Arthur Christopher
Benson's *Leaves of the Tree,* written in our
own time. As I was reading with intense
pleasure Mr. Benson's book, it came over
me that we had in America men not only
of equal interior power, but also of equal
personal charm, worthy of a similar chron-
icle; and I wondered if we were going to
allow their unique traits to be forgotten. In
spite of an impression to the contrary, we in
America are far more reticent than our
brave English allies: it is painfully difficult

for us to speak of the ideals and the heroes about whom we care most. We are possibly a little too sensitive to ridicule. We imagine the smiling critic as he takes up our imaginary volume—we think we hear him murmur, "All very well, this book; but it ought to be called, 'Great Men Who have Known Me.'" And forthwith, though we have reverently touched the hem of the garments of the saints, we allow the fragrant memory of them to fade from the earth.

Most of the names commemorated in this book are well known. Two or three will be strange to almost every reader: I have included them because they represent a group of striking personalities of such real power that they would stand among the renowned of the earth if the appeal of a conspicuous opportunity had come to them, and also because they are the sort of people who inspire others to attainment and to action, while they themselves prefer a dimmer light. One of the heroes is a boy, his life here finished

before its promise had been tested: these are
days when we know the greatness of youth,
and exalt the glory of the unfinished. We
suspect to what famous tasks the Master of
All the Worlds has assigned them in the
blessed Country to which they have gone.

As one generation passes and another be-
gins, we, who have known the old leaders,
lament that those who are to lead the future
did not know face to face the men who inspired us. I remember that once in a college
class-room the lecturer broke off from his
subject with the remark that, when he was
a young man, he and his friends were constantly looking forward to a new poem by
Browning or Tennyson or Matthew Arnold,
a new essay by Carlyle, or a new novel by
Thackeray; and he wondered how we of a
duller age could have any courage or spirit
without the incentive which had been his.
There is a benevolent motive, therefore, in
the attempt to prolong the lives of our heroes
and saints. We would have them flash, if

only for an instant, their radiant faces upon
the oncoming generation.

C. L. S.

GRACE CHURCH RECTORY,
    NEW YORK,
      12 *October,* 1918.

ACKNOWLEDGMENTS

UNDER the name of Romney Reynolds the chapter in this book on Josiah Royce was published in The Outlook and several of the other sketches were printed in The Churchman. To the Editors of these magazines grateful acknowledgment is made.

Thanks are due also to those who have allowed the reproduction of photographs and paintings for the illustrations, especially to Dr. Mixter, the friend of Bishop Brooks, who took the intimate photograph which is the frontispiece, and to Mrs. Rieber, who has just completed for Harvard University the remarkable painting of The Three Harvard Philosophers.

CONTENTS

I. PHILLIPS BROOKS 3

II. ANDREW PRESTON PEABODY 19

III. WILLIAM JAMES 33

IV. JOSIAH ROYCE 51

V. ALEXANDER VIETS GRISWOLD ALLEN . 67

VI. HENRY SYLVESTER NASH 85

VII. BISHOP WHIPPLE 101

VIII. TWO COUSINS BY MARRIAGE 117

IX. A BOY I KNEW 131

X. A MINNESOTA DOCTOR 147

XI. SAMUEL HART 161

XII. HENRY VAUGHAN 175

XIII. A PENNSYLVANIA HOME 187

XIV. BISHOP HARE 207

XV. WILLIAM REED HUNTINGTON . . . 225

LIST OF ILLUSTRATIONS

FACING
PAGE

PHILLIPS BROOKS in his Study. From a Photograph by Dr. S. J. Mixter.. *Frontispiece*

ANDREW PRESTON PEABODY. From a Photograph by Pach....................   22

WILLIAM JAMES, JOSIAH ROYCE, and PROFESSOR PALMER. From a Painting by Winifred Rieber.....................   40

ALEXANDER VIETS GRISWOLD ALLEN in his Study. From a Photograph..........   74

HENRY SYLVESTER NASH. From a Painting by Wilton Lockwood.................   88

BISHOP WHIPPLE. From a Photograph.... 108

MARY JOANNA WHIPPLE. From a Photograph............................... 120

MARY WEBSTER WHIPPLE. From a Photograph............................... 126

A BOY I KNEW. From a Photograph by C. N. Peterson...................... 134

CHARLES NATHANIEL HEWITT. From a Painting by his Son.................. 150

SAMUEL HART. From a Photograph...... 166

HENRY VAUGHAN, From a Photograph.... 178

FACING
PAGE

FELIX REVILLE BRUNOT. From a Photograph by F. Gutekunst............... 190

MARY BRUNOT. From a Photograph by
H. Bower........................... 200

BISHOP HARE. From a Photograph by
Elmer Chickering, Boston............ 210

WILLIAM REED HUNTINGTON. From a Photograph by Henry Havelock Pierce, Boston and New York................... 230

CERTAIN AMERICAN FACES

PHILLIPS BROOKS

PHILLIPS BROOKS

I CANNOT remember when first I heard the name of Phillips Brooks. As a boy I recognized that his name stood for distinction. When I decided to go to Harvard College an affectionate old bishop shook his head, saying that he wished I wouldn't—for he thought it quite likely that my boyish faith would shrivel and die in a rationalistic atmosphere. It wasn't my father's college, but I had made up my mind that I was meant to go to Harvard. I was thousands of miles away from Cambridge when I was pushing my decision through. I wanted reinforcement. It suddenly occurred to me that Phillips Brooks would tell me the whole truth about the matter, and, though I had never seen him, I wrote him a letter.

I suppose it was a crude, boyish letter. I have often wondered what I said and how I said it. But I cannot recall a single line. Doubtless the letter lay one morning on Mr. Brooks's table in Clarendon Street with a score or two of other morning letters. The other letters were probably from English bishops, or American poets, or important vestrymen, or statesmen, or writers. They probably said grateful words about some sermon, or sought counsel on serious problems of life. But, if one may judge from the quickness with which the answer came, the strange boy's letter must have been answered that very morning with the first. It was no brief conventional reference to a catalogue or a college tract; it was the simple, straight assurance that one must expect to find in Harvard College what one would find in the world—scoffing, perhaps blaspheming, but also earnest Christian faith and effort; and he advised the boy to come with the hope of being a better Christian man for having gone through Harvard College. And then he added, "Come and see me when you are settled in Cambridge."

I showed the letter to a beloved teacher. "Do you know," he said, "what that letter means? Do you know how busy that man is? Do you know that he has given you his best?" I didn't then know what the best of Phillips Brooks was, but I knew that the letter was wonderful. I read it over and over, and I was sure that Harvard College was for me.

From that time till he died Phillips Brooks was my revered master—though, kind as he was whenever I spoke with him face to face, I never dared to follow him except from afar. Whenever I could, I went to hear him preach, or speak in less formal ways; and I stood off in some obscure corner to look at him when he plunged through the college yard, or rose above a crowd of listeners at a public meeting, or strode down a Boston street. He instantly seemed the one man I had known who could take a legitimate place with Plato and Dante and other greatest men of all time.

The first Sunday morning of the term I made my way to Trinity Church in Boston. The church was thronged, and I was given a seat back of the pulpit somewhere in the depths of the chancel. I saw Phillips Brooks for the first time; I heard him read swiftly and reverently the familiar service. I felt the thrill of the vast responding congregation. But when the preacher mounted the pulpit and preached his sermon, I couldn't hear a word. I knew that a torrent of words was going forth from him, and I knew that hundreds of people who were in front of him were being stirred to the bottom of their souls. But, bitterly disappointed, I was as one outside the sound of his voice. That night he came to Appleton Chapel with Edward Everett Hale, Dr. George Gordon, and others, making one of the short addresses. I heard him then; but

the address, though earnest, was slight; and
I still felt that I had not heard Phillips
Brooks preach.

There was no lack of opportunity as the
years passed. How many of his sermons
and addresses I heard, I cannot tell; but I
know that he fed my spirit as no other. I
felt the goodness and the love of God as
I never expected to know them. Through
him I seemed to know intimately the Christ
who was to him evidently the most real of
Masters. I knew that he was yearning to
win the people, known and unknown, before
him, to a discipleship like his own. I did
not feel at once the need of going to see
him, though he was easily approached, and
he had definitely invited me to come; I suspect that I found in his public utterance
the unconscious telling of his own experience. I looked up to his big eyes and caught
their friendliness for humanity, and was con-
tent to be lost in a sort of anonymous friendship.

No doubt the physical presence had much to do with the impression which he was then forcing upon young men. It was not only because he was big, though that had its effect. When he stood alone in a pulpit he did not seem uncommonly tall, because he was big in every way. Every feature of his face and person was proportionally big, so that, unless one compared him with others, he seemed quite normal. The power came from a beauty, a sweetness, a light, which radiated from his face whether in repose or in appeal. It was the fineness and integrity of character which found in his huge form scope for interpretation: that is what made Phillips Brooks a joy to earnest youth seeking a guide for life at its best.

The day came at length when I gathered courage to go to see him, when he kept office hours in the preacher's room at Harvard. I waited my turn on a bench in the hall of Wadsworth House, feeling more and more wretchedly aware that I hadn't anything to

say to the great man. But the caller before
me came out of the preacher's room to tell
me that Mr. Brooks was ready for the next
visitor. And in I tumbled, to find an
enormous hand closed over mine, and a
mountain of a man smiling down into my
timid face. As soon as I sat down I thanked
him for the letter he had written me; he
remembered all about it, and gradually pried
open the shy speech that clung somewhere
in my throat. He asked about a building
in a distant city which we both knew. I
ventured to say that it was a copy from
something in Canada. Then he put his head
back and laughed. I said they might tear
it down. Whereupon he pointed out the
expense, and told me of a window by La
Farge in Trinity Church. Mr. and Mrs.
La Farge came to see it. Said Mrs. La
Farge, "My dear, you can't afford to leave
it." Then Mr. La Farge answered with a
groan, "That's just it, my dear; I can't
afford to take it out." Whereupon Mr.

Brooks's big head went back again, and we laughed together. I don't believe there was anything important said; only I carried away an impression of kindness, and I was sure that if I really needed him, I could go to Phillips Brooks and find him aware of me, and caring. I heard and saw this spacious person henceforth with a sense of ownership. He knew me just a little; and every day I was getting deeper and deeper into him.

The years passed, and I decided definitely to prepare for the Ministry. I spoke to him about a theological seminary quite far from Harvard in place and spirit. I said I thought it might be wise to let myself be broadened by a new atmosphere. Whereupon he jumped up, and glaring down at me, said sharply, "Don't you think you'd better get the truth?" It was a flash from the magnificent rage which was always burning beneath his kindness and cheer. I saw it once at a college dinner when a suave toastmaster said that there was one man present whom he had promised not to ask to speak, but the other guests were under no promise and could do as they liked—his name was Phillips Brooks. Whereupon Colonel Lee and other very old alumni leaped to their feet; instantly all the rest rose to join them in applause, which continued till Mr. Brooks was compelled to stand up. In the hush that followed he cast such a look upon the toastmaster as I think I never saw on any face before or since. "You told me you wouldn't," he said in a husky voice—and I think we all grew pale, not quite knowing what the giant might do with the culprit who sat across the room at the head of the speakers' table. Then, pulling himself together, he said calmly, "Well, I must say something;" and went on to recount the impression made on him by the fine speeches which had gone before. It was the memorable speech of a memorable occasion. He was a volcano in perfect control;

occasionally he let the fiery lava have its way.

Once again I was to see him in such a humour, with the revelation of its meaning. In due time he became a bishop, and I was one of his candidates for the Ministry. He took us all very seriously, insisting that we write him four letters a year, telling him about ourselves; sometimes when he visited the theological school he would see us one by one alone. He asked me, on one of these visits, how the Ministry seemed to me, now that I was definitely pledged to it. I said, honestly, that I felt its great responsibility. I suppose I looked a bit downhearted. In any case he came over to me, as if by violence he were going to shake me out of such a mood: "But don't you see the joy of it?" he demanded. I then knew the meaning of these indignant flashes: they were the index of how much he cared.

After all, however, it is not the memory of his letters and personal conversation which

I cherish most. The debt I owe him is from those sacred moments when I sat with hundreds of others and heard him preach. I went to the Convention that elected him bishop; I shared the exultation and the indignation which all the youth of the neighbourhood felt in that summer of strange opposition and misunderstanding. I saw him stand in Trinity Church to receive his commission as bishop. Who that saw him rise from among the seated congregation as Bishop Potter gave him the charge can forget the glory of self-forgetfulness shining in his beautiful face! After that I went to hear him in London, in Boston, and in Massachusetts villages—and I saw that he was constantly weary, so weary that he would often stumble as he read his sermons. I wondered if the power were waning. And then I heard him during his last Lent, every Monday in St. Paul's, Boston; on those Monday noons he seemed to be beyond his previous best in the confidence of his Christian faith, in the winning power of its presentation. He afterwards confessed that these addresses cost him more than anything he ever had done; yet we with the airy notions of youth thought he was tossing them off on the spur of the moment. He was dying, though probably not even he knew it. He was working too hard. He was, like his Master, eager that men should live, and live more abundantly. It was a consuming love which shone through his incessant preaching. It was the supreme expression of love which the Saviour praised.

On a Monday in January, 1893, we of a certain theological seminary were going about our work as usual when the word came that Phillips Brooks was dead. We were stunned. We couldn't believe it. We wandered aimlessly from room to room to ask each other how it could be. We told each other all we could say about his sermons, his personal conversations, his character. We knew as we never had known before who

he was. All the impressions of the past were
gathered into one massive whole, and we
were aware of a stupendous personality.
The machinery of the school stopped for the
week. We went to his funeral; all Massachusetts seemed either in Trinity Church or
in Copley Square; thousands upon thousands of people seemed to have one heart,
and that was bleeding for its noble friend
and counsellor. Some of us reached by accident the Harvard Yard just as his body
was being borne through the ranks of bare-
headed students lined up to do honour to
the greatest alumnus of the university.

That was Thursday. On Thursday afternoons in those days there was a Vesper
Service in Appleton Chapel. I happened
to remember the service and went to it.
Several of the college preachers were there
to share the service; Dr. George Gordon
went up into the pulpit. I remember still
how my heart sank as I thought of his task
that afternoon. "What can he say to us,"

I said to myself, "what can he say to young men who feel that their chief teacher and inspiration is withdrawn from their sight?" In perfect simplicity Dr. Gordon said the best word any one could have said. "If," he concluded, "it was a great thing to have known Phillips Brooks, think what it must be to know Phillips Brooks's Master!" I am sure that is what Phillips Brooks would most have liked to have him say, for Phillips Brooks gave himself to preach Christ to men. As we went away in the darkness of that bleak January evening we were comforted, more convinced than ever that a life like that of our dear leader could not stop on any Monday in any January, that its enormous energy and affection had burst the bonds of death, and was alive for evermore in the eternal Christ for whom and in whom he lived.

ANDREW PRESTON PEABODY

ANDREW PRESTON PEABODY

THERE are faces so familiar to one's memory that it seems impossible to believe that one has never spoken to their owners. When I was an undergraduate at Harvard College I suppose the most revered figure who passed in and out of the college yard was Andrew Preston Peabody. I fancy that the first time we saw him we knew instinctively who he was. The smiling face in which shone rare goodness as well as benevolence, was a stay against freshman pessimism, and I suspect it held many a youth, inclined to be wild, from his sin. He was very old. He had ceased to teach, and a sermon or lecture was an infrequent task. He continued to live in the house near the Library which was one of the perquisites of the Plummer Professor, and so was seldom absent from the college precincts. The merest stroll brought him face to face with the successive generations of students of the University. He was, in a way, to all kinds of men, the embodiment of Harvard College. And yet few of us had ever spoken to him.

Only a year or two before my day, "compulsory chapel" had ceased, and the voluntary system (largely under the inspiration of Phillips Brooks) had begun. All sorts of anecdotes clustered around the head of our ancient hero. It was said that in the old days of compulsory prayers, if the Plummer Professor (who was the Chaplain and who regularly conducted Prayers and preached) was caught preaching beyond a certain fixed time, the Chapel was filled with gentle tappings, which came from hundreds of feet, accidentally touching the wood of the pews in front of them. There was also a rumour that once in a prayer he had said, "Paradoxical as it may seem to thee, O

Lord, it is nevertheless perfectly clear to us. . . . " And his courses in moral philosophy had been what the collegian of that day vulgarly called "snaps"—that is, courses of lectures easy and pleasant to listen to; and if a man could get a good mark in any course, he was fairly sure to win it from this kindest of readers of examination blue books.

There were lingering tales of the older days of Cambridge. On a very hot day Dr. Oliver Wendell Holmes was making his way across the Cambridge Common. With hat in hand he was drying his wet forehead with his handkerchief. And so he met Dr. Peabody, who, in his chronic absent-mindedness, did not recognize his friend; but he saw the hat, and, assuming a beggar, with notions of charity not then outworn, he dropped a few small coins into it, and passed on. At another time, when cows were wont to ramble on Cambridge streets, he one day awoke from his absent-minded dreaming to recog-

nize that he had just passed a lady to whom
he had neglected to bow. "I must not be
so rude again," he said to himself. In a few
minutes some students saw the genial man
wave his hat gallantly to a passing cow. Very
absurd and trifling tales were these; but they
served as pegs on which young men could
hang their affection for the venerable saint.

I can remember only one time when I
heard him preach. The old vigour for which
he had been known was gone, but the sweetness was as winning as ever. I cannot remember a word he said that evening in the
forlorn old Appleton Chapel, but I can remember the kind eyes looking out through
the square gold spectacles. I can even
remember that he had added something to
his manuscript on a certain page. I felt
sure that it was a page preached many times,
with many notes, between lines, in margins,
and on the back. In any case he was evidently looking for a sentence which viciously
eluded his search. Without the least em-

ANDREW PRESTON PEABODY.

barrassment he held the leaf up to his dear old eyes, turned the paper first to one side, then to the other, and finally upside down; there he found the straying sentence, and joyfully read it, with slow emphasis, to a waiting congregation. I dare say that, even at ten o'clock that night, we could not have told much about the sermon; but we all knew that it had done us good.

Those were days when an institution known as "the College Conference" was in vogue, because the authorities wished to make sure that the rapidly growing numbers were not too seriously separating the undergraduates from the faculty. Therefore eminent men gave informal talks in "Sever Eleven" on appointed nights, and afterwards, sitting back, invited any student in the throngs who came to ask questions or talk back. It was an effort to cultivate intimacy by wholesale. President Eliot came one night. He told of a graduate who advised him not to recommend a classmate for a certain responsible position. "He isn't an honest man," said the complacent Pharisee; "he used to write my themes for me when we were in college." Dr. Lyman Abbott came, explaining his theological system. A weird student in the top row asked Dr. Abbott plaintively if he were not a Eutychian. "I have no interest," said Dr. Abbott, "in those ancient distinctions. I don't know what a Eutychian is." "I thought so," said the student with a sigh—which put the whole crowd into a roar of laughter. Colonel Thomas Wentworth Higginson came, and talked of Literature as a Profession. He told of Thoreau, commanded by his publishers to remove from their shop one thousand copies of "The Maine Woods," which wouldn't sell. At dusk the weary author, too poor to employ a boy to carry the books for him, sat down in his attic on the last pile of "The Maine Woods" which he had brought up the stairs, whipped out his diary, and wrote, "I am now the possessor of a library of twelve hundred volumes—one thousand of which I wrote myself." That was the courage needed for a man who made literature his profession. Governor Wolcott (not yet Governor) came, at the request of the faculty, to explain why the unpopular decree had gone forth that every student must report at some convenient place every morning at nine o'clock. This was to make sure that men who had unusual freedom began their day betimes. It was a hostile body of students which glared down at the handsome face behind the desk. Professor Royce afterwards said that the superb beauty of the pleader was what won the rebellious audience to think that after all it was a wise faculty which required grown men to say, "I'm up, Sir," at nine o'clock in the morning. Dr. Peabody came—and I can't remember his subject or a single word he said! I remember only the benign face, beaming upon us all: and I remember the reverent hush upon the hundreds of men who filled every inch of the big room. I think we did not expect to hear much, for we knew that the old man's work was done; but we brought our reverence and love, and laid them at his feet. The fact that we knew enough to be proud of him, and that we cared enough to let him know it, was what that evening meant; and we saw the face—always the face—filled with joy and peace.

Among those of us who dipped into theology, it was always explained that Dr. Andrew Peabody was not really a Unitarian. He belonged to that almost vanished wing of Unitarianism which simply revolted against the heresy of tritheism in Calvinism. We found him wholly orthodox in his allegiance to the Person of Christ. Later I was to read his essay on the Fourth Gospel, which was published with essays by Bishop Lightfoot and Dr. E. A. Abbot on the same subject. It is twenty-five years and more since I have seen the book: but I still recall one page in Dr. Peabody's essay. Con-

vinced as he was that the Gospel was written
by St. John the Beloved Disciple, he sought
in his own experience a reason for the vivid-
ness of the details. How—people had asked
—could a very old man, like the traditional
author, have remembered such trifling incidents as he had recorded, which had happened perhaps seventy years before? Dr.
Peabody said that he could understand it all;
for in his own old age he was remembering incidents of his youth and early manhood more
clearly than events which had happened in
all the years since then. The book seemed
to him like an old man's book. I have read
many books and essays on the Fourth Gospel and its authorship; but I have never read
anything which seemed quite so real a contribution to the difficult controversy. For
he was a Beloved Disciple himself, and his
"heart had reasons which the reason cannot
know."

The last time I saw Dr. Andrew Peabody
was at a college dinner, made up of older

alumni with only a few younger men. One of the chief guests was Bishop Potter, who, I think, had just received a Harvard degree. Dr. Peabody, in his brief and simple speech, had referred to the days when "the reverend Bishop's honoured father" was Rector of St. Paul's, Boston; for it was young Peabody's custom to walk into Boston on Sunday afternoons to hear Dr. Alonzo Potter preach. When it came Bishop Potter's turn to speak, he told of a frequent experience after the Sunday morning service when he was Rector of Grace Church, New York. "That person," he said, "who exercises the most constant and critical watchfulness over my preaching would say to me, 'Henry, you've been at it again!' 'At what, my dear?' I would say. 'You've been reading Dr. Andrew Peabody's sermons again!'" The Bishop straightened himself during the laughter; and then added, "Gentlemen, I had!" As every one clapped, Dr. Peabody wept with affectionate gratitude for the

finely turned praise. Then Bishop Potter
grew very serious. "I often hear," he said,
"discussions about Harvard College, with
harsh criticisms of its rash freedom, its pro-
verbial indifference, its worldliness; but I
always say that as long as the Harvard
undergraduate looks up to Andrew Peabody
as the typical Harvard graduate, and re-
veres him as the finest fruit of the university life, Harvard College is safe."

That is a judgment which every Harvard
alumnus of that period would gratefully
echo. Though I never spoke to Dr. Andrew
Peabody, and he never spoke to me, I keep
his photograph among some other photographs which I like to look at from time
to time. But had I no such symbol, I should
yet remember, as if I had seen it only yester-
day, the face of an old man, who had bravely
and lovingly lived his life; who, without
bitterness or envy, saw other men doing his
work; and who faced with joy the coming
of the new and brighter day.

WILLIAM JAMES

WILLIAM JAMES

BEFORE William James had, through the publishing of his Psychology, become great to the world he was great to his pupils in Harvard College. Even those who touched his life less intimately than in the class-room felt the amazing charm of his personality. We told one another stories of his skill in being frank and kind, as we experienced his honesty and his brotherly love; and we were proud that he belonged to us and we to him. It has been reported that his friends were somewhat impatient because he was constantly finding the thesis of some immature pupil wonderful. We, poor things, didn't know how many geniuses he was discovering along the dull pathway of life; and for days we trod on air, because he, the cleverest man we knew, had found something original and striking in our first essay at philosophical thought: we thereupon speculated how far we might go from such a brave start. It was not only that we appreciated him; we listened gaily to one who had the rare discernment to appreciate us!

I can't remember that I ever heard in college days a certain story his brother later, in a book, told of the boyhood of William James; but I know how we should have gloated over it had we known it then. This story was of an afternoon when William was going off for an excursion with his particular cronies; and Henry, a trifle younger, wished to go too. William tried all sorts of dissuasion, but Henry pathetically pleaded that he must not be left behind. When everything else failed, William saw that imagination alone could help; so he drew near to Henry with wild eyes, and said in a ghostly voice, "No, Henry, you can't

go; for the boys *I* go with curse and swear."
That settled it; Henry knew that he himself
kept no such company—so he stayed at
home. One instantly sees how the psychologist could have surpassed the novelist
at his fiction.

How, too, we should have exulted over
the story, now known, of his first choice of
a life-work. He decided to be a painter, and
put himself to learn under William Chase.
One day he turned sharply to his master and
said, "Mr. Chase, shall I ever paint great
pictures?" "No," was the answer; "you will
paint very good pictures, but not great."
"Very well," said the pupil; "I won't paint
any." And he turned away to medicine and
psychology and the inspiration of youth;
thus he found the work of his life.

I doubt if the ordinary interpretation of
such a story would have seemed to us true.
He would seek a work which he could do
eminently, we should have said, not for his
own sake, but for the sake of his fellows:

he would have liked to do his best by the world. For there was about him a blithe unconsciousness of self; a crowding interest in his subject, a generous appreciation of others. I have heard that at home he was wont to ask everyone else to stop speaking, that one member of his household could be fully and completely understood: "What was that —— said? Listen!" He most of all wished to hear. His was the gift of self-forgetful admiration.

We never tired of telling one another how one day he was standing before a blackboard demonstrating some large truth, cantering as it were through open fields, and easily leaping every barrier. We felt that he was going to solve what we had thought never could be solved. Then suddenly he stopped. "That is as far as I can see," he said; and sat down. There was about him a transparent candour which won us heart and soul. He never glided over difficulties or pretended to know what he did not know.

His absolute truthfulness sometimes made trying situations, of which he was often quite unconscious at the time. He was once invited to deliver at a woman's club in Somerville a paper which he had prepared for the young women of Radcliffe College. Towards the end, absorbed in his task, he read, "And now, my fair hearers——" Suddenly he checked himself with the very serious explanation, "Oh, that wasn't meant for *you!*" A woman in the back of the room was heard to say under her breath, "He might have spared us that."

The chapter on Habit in his Psychology is commonly placed among the finest lay sermons ever preached. He now and then dropped advice in his lectures which showed the same grasp upon the practical use of philosophy. He had a way of stripping off the conventional excuses and evasions, and putting the inevitable consequences of certain acts or habits in their exact light. He was more than a teacher of youth; he was a guide.

One of his sons once told me how his father despised stamp-collecting; as he looked down upon the small heads of his boys absorbed over a stamp-album, he would murmur with contempt, "The nasty little things!" He was giving his pupils a similar sense of proportion. My first sense of the greatness of Franz Hals was when Mr. James hung in one of the philosophical lecture rooms a fine photograph of one of Hals's portraits. He was always opening the windows of life for us. Having shown his sons what he thought of their stamps, he straightway went to Boston to buy them more!

His consideration for others knew no bounds. My friend and classmate, Henry Washburn, was minded during his theological course to seek his counsel on a thesis he was writing on The Priority of Faith as a Method of Discovering the Truth, and

accordingly presented himself at Mr.
James's door. The maid hesitated, but at
last, admitting him, led him up two flights
of stairs to a barely furnished attic room.
Even the walls were unfinished. It was
evidently Mr. James's desert to which he
could retreat from the conventional world.
The great philosopher, in his wrapper, was
sitting in an old wooden rocking chair, his
feet in another chair, swathed in blankets,
a picture of wool and of misery. But he
was delighted to have the human touch, and
joyously began his tale. "You can't
imagine," he began, "how I came into this
plight. A pedlar came along the other day
with what he called 'The Elixir of Life';
and he talked so beguilingly about it that
I bought a bottle of him. And this," he
added with a twinge, "is the result." And
then he discoursed on the priority of faith
as a method of discovering the truth. He
knew!

A conspicuous element in his charm was

his quick humour. Several students were one night dining with him. As they went out of the dining room, Mr. James suggested that everyone do something to amuse the rest. So one said that he would sing; another, that he would impersonate a famous actor; all made their pledges but one. This man lingered behind with Mr. James, saying with a blush, "You know, Mr. James, I have no parlour tricks." Instantly Mr. James put his hand affectionately over the fellow's shoulder: "Neither have I," he whispered confidentially—"but then you know there must be some onions in the soup." The humour was fused with kindness.

And how kind he could be! Towards the end of my college course I decided to try for Honours in Philosophy. The first requirement was a thesis written in a single day upon a subject given in the morning. I went to Professor Palmer's house at half-past ten, and was given three subjects from which I chose "A Doctrine of Conscience."

From a painting by Winifred Rieber.

George Herbert Palmer.
William James.

THE HARVARD PHILOSOPHERS.

Josiah Royce.

After a day of rapid writing I carried the finished thesis, at nine at night, to the same door. All the professors in the philosophical department were to read it. At length it came back to me with a note saying that the thesis was satisfactory, and I could present myself for the oral examination. That was pleasant; but the pleasantest part of it was that I found written across the cover of the thesis, "I say Yes to this!—W. J." I felt that a friendly hand was held out. A few afternoons later I entered a Cambridge study where all the philosophical professors were gathered. I was the only candidate, and I fancy everyone was sorry for me, as I came in to be bound to the stake and burned. The tension was loosened by a laugh from William James, with, "Here comes our victim!" One after another put questions to me about the men or the principles which particularly interested him. I have forgotten nearly all the questions; but one of them I shall never forget. "Was

Descartes first of all a physicist or a metaphysicist?" asked Mr. James. "Oh," I answered easily, "a metaphysicist." Mr. James looked at me anxiously, as if he were so impressed with my learning that he might revise his knowledge; but he said at length, "Yes, one would think so, wouldn't one?—but, you know, as a matter of fact, he wasn't." Was ever a confident neophyte let down more gently! I am quite sure that he gave to his learned colleagues the impression that it was more intelligent to be overwhelmed by an enthusiasm for Descartes' metaphysical importance than to know the humdrum fact that Descartes spent most of his time doing something else. From that moment my admiration for William James passed over into love.

Yet after that I rarely saw him. My home was to be far from Cambridge. Now and then I had a letter from him with the same aptness of phrase, the same kindness, the same humour; though I was only one of the thousands who touched his life, he let me know that he did not forget. Thenceforth I was to be his pupil more than ever, but it was through his books, which he then began to publish with frequency. I could imagine how he said the words which I read on the printed page. His personality illumined his marvellous literary style.

It was a red letter day when I sat down to read *The Will to Believe*. That he chose the essay with this title to give its name to the whole book revealed a dominant characteristic: he himself had the will to believe. A good many hopes and confidences which his neighbours had, were not his; but he sympathethically studied them, and there was no trace of scorn for the faith of others. He had the will to believe all things glad and beautiful; and the richness of his own nature grew before us, as we watched him standing with upturned face towards the sun. It was like him to tell the story of Henry IV and Crillon after a great victory,

when Henry cried to his tardy general,
"Hang yourself, brave Crillon! we fought at
Arques, and you were not there." To
William James life was a victory at which
he exulted to be present, and he liked to
catch the victorious emotions of those who
fought at his side.

Then came *The Varieties of Religious
Experience.* Here we saw his profoundly
religious nature; for he spoke with respect
of the abnormal and emotional types which
would most often be disregarded by professional thinkers. One couldn't help feeling
that the normal type, as shown in the
development of Christian theology, was not
sufficiently described; and one would deduce
more theology than Professor James de-
duced from the mass of Christian experience; but nothing could blind one to the
reverent enthusiasm for the varied ways in
which God made Himself known to men.
His pupils did not need to be assured that
James was one of the most religious men

of his time; but they rejoiced that the world also, through this book, recognized the fact.

It puzzled him when any of his pupils, aroused to religious fervour by his teaching and example, turned for ultimate satisfaction to association with organized Christianity. While his colleague and friend, Professor Royce, was steadily increasing his devotion to the idea of a Beloved Community as the goal of religion, Professor James was increasingly sure that all high experiences must come to the individual man absolutely alone. He once said to a young woman, "Why do you tie yourself up to the rules and conventions of a very conservative Church, when you are by nature the freest and most spontaneous creature I know?" She answered simply that in the very best thing she knew in life she liked to share the happiness and the help of it. She said that she couldn't imagine religion without fellowship. He was much interested and gave his usual rapt attention as if he were about to be converted; but he said at length: "Well, religion is for me an individual matter. When I think of religion I think of a desolate heath in the silence of the night; the cold wind is blowing over my bald head; one star is shining; and I have the conviction of utter isolation."

Towards the end, we read his expositions of Pragmatism. This doctrine seemed to those who had known him years before in the class-room, thoroughly consistent with his whole life. Brilliant men came then to Harvard College (as they have always come to universities) often to go so deeply into speculative thought that they never struck out to do anything for the world. If they went to such waste it was in spite of William James; for he was the most practical of philosophers. He put all his theories, discoveries, and principles to work, and they shone every morning in his face and in his quivering action. It was not only truth which he sought, but truth expressed in life. The conservative shook their heads: they shuddered for the fate of the ideal and the absolute. All that was whimsical and adventurous came out in James's chivalrous defence of Pragmatism; and he did the world of theology and philosophy unmeasured good thereby. A hard logic, a mathematical correctness, did not appear any longer the only goal of reflection. Men bowed their heads and remembered One who said, "By their fruits ye shall know them." James was holding up to thought a test which has divine sanction.

One day in London, in the Summer of 1910, I picked up a morning *Times* to read that William James was dead. I could not believe that one who seemed, when last I saw him, young and radiant, could have finished his earthly career. And sitting there, alone in a great city, I mourned him. It was consolation to find in the chief daily paper of the world, far from his home, several solid columns of appreciation of the man who lived a quiet scholar's life in the American Cambridge. Evidently, after all I was not alone in a strange land; for there were men in all the earth who longed to read words of gratitude and praise for William James. He was a master who had gained the love even of those who never saw his face.

JOSIAH ROYCE

JOSIAH ROYCE

I FIRST saw Josiah Royce somewhat more than thirty years ago. I had been living in the far West, and Chicago proved to be the most convenient place for me to take my entrance examinations for Harvard College. One hot July morning, forty or fifty boys from various parts of the West, most of them wholly strangers to all the others, climbed the stairs of a school building on the North Side. On the top floor we found the room appointed for our examinations. Breezes came in at the windows, and also great flakes of soot which blackened our hands, and our blue books— on which the examinations were written. We waited nervously for the examiner from Cambridge. A large person with bushy side-whiskers came in. Sudden silence fell on the room: evidently this was the executioner. But he passed the platform, sat down at a little desk next mine, and took out twelve wonderfully sharpened pencils. There was a rustle of relief, as we all took breath again. Just a moment before the hour announced there appeared a short man with a large head, looking as we who had read Greek history thought Socrates must have looked: he carried a leather bag, which he put down on the big platform desk, and then sat solemnly behind it. He frankly looked us over, and we gazed at him; he seemed human and humorous and kind. Things didn't seem so bad after all. This was Josiah Royce.

I can remember only one sentence which he said in those anxious hot July days. Someone went to the desk to ask him a question. Evidently he felt that whatever information was imparted must be given to all: so we heard him say quite clearly in his quizzical voice, as his eyes rested on a tall chimney outside the window: "You want to know what is meant by 'the composition of a word.' Well, the composition of mortar is lime and sand and water." We began to think that if we ever did do so foolish a thing as to study philosophy (for by this time we had pried out of one of our number, who had a Harvard Catalogue, that the inquisitor taught philosophy), we shouldn't mind attaching ourselves to one of his classes. These were days when the elective system was at the height of its newly discovered glory, and we had a sense of unusual freedom as we inspected the faculty and their wares.

For three years I resisted the impulse to elect one of his courses. I saw him constantly, and felt a sense of ownership in the various anecdotes about him and his small boy, which the students told one another. This was the boy who thwarted an afternoon tea by tying crape to the door-bell, and who, in sprinkling the grass, and seeing a delightfully infirm old man amble by, turned the hose on Mr. James Russell Lowell, who thereupon gave up his call on Mr. Charles Eliot Norton, and was carefully tended by the boy's anxious parents. My only memory of this brilliant boy was meeting him one afternoon at the college pump, where a group of students were slaking their thirst. I asked the boy if he didn't want me to pump some water for him, whereupon he answered with a musical drawl, very slowly, "No, I-do-not-want-you-to-pump-my-waw-taw; I-will-pump-my-own-wawtaw." We talked of our Socrates, as he made his way back and forth through the college yard; and we were proud of him and of the binding force of our university; for he resisted a very loud and lucrative call from the newly established University of Chicago, preferring bread and water and the companionship of William James and George Herbert Palmer to milk and honey without them.

In my senior year I sat under Professor

Royce in a stiff course on the History of
German Thought from 1770 to 1830. It
was a course which brought out the rich
variety of Royce's learning and culture. He
discussed the two Fausts of Goethe; most
of us learned for the first time through his
exposition of Herder what was meant by the
modern historical method; we tried to follow
him as he told us what Kant meant in the
pages of the *Kritik* which we had read (or
thought we read) the night before; we loved
Fichte; we laughed at Heine; we revelled in
Hegel, and found out how much more we
knew than he in the end. The difficulty and
the charm went side by side; and though we
knew that we were listening to more than we
could appropriate, some of the insight and
the wisdom sank in, and has become a large
part of the foundation of whatever earnest
thinking we have done since.

It was in this same year that he gave in
Sanders Theatre some popular lectures,
which were afterwards published as *The*

Spirit of Modern Philosophy. The ground covered was largely the ground covered in his college lectures, and most of us went to view the landscape from this slightly different angle. He had an inspiring way of quoting the Bible, illuminating by his context a familiar passage, which seemed to say exactly what the philosopher of the evening wished to say and couldn't. The ladies of Cambridge, who made up most of the audience, understood these happy quotations. Now and then there would be a flash of humour, as when he described the boy learning to write, who grasped the pen in his tight fist, and then put his tongue in his cheek, and at length wrote. The ladies of Cambridge nodded to one another over these sallies, and understood perfectly how delightful philosophy was. But for the most part, when the lecturer sailed the seas where no figure or illustration could float, there was evident discouragement on most of the faces; and we who had the privilege of having learned the sage's style went back to our rooms to laugh impertinently because the ladies of Cambridge were taking externally a course in philosophy. Well, it was something to have said that one had been present at these memorable lectures.

After my graduation, while I was in a professional school, I took another of Professor Royce's courses. This was on Cosmology, and showed in an amazing way his familiarity with Science. The basis of the course was Spencer's book, *First Principles,* which he mercilessly criticized. We read also, among many other books, Joseph Le Conte's *Evolution,* which he always referred to with affection. I think Le Conte had been an old teacher in Royce's early life in California. The whole course turned on the fact that because there was an unknown element in life, it was not therefore unknowable; that even if we could not know all, what we did know in part, we did know; and that there were two methods of knowing: one by description (like mathematics) and the other by appreciation (like poetry, love, patriotism). We who had known the Royce of Goethe, Kant, Fichte, and Hegel found a new Royce in this course. In some ways we saw more deeply into his wisdom, perhaps because we were getting more deeply into the knowledge of the man.

Pragmatism had not then found definite expression, but in his devotion to the Absolute, Royce was even then ready for the fray which was later to engage him. One morning he began to describe an angel who said that by his experience two and two make five. There was a pause. We expected that Royce would go on to explain that there might conceivably be a consciousness quite unlike our earth-consciousness in which two and two *would* make five. But we were brought suddenly to our senses. "If," said Royce fiercely, "I met that angel—I'd know what sort of an angel that was!"

It was at about this time, when he was giv-

ing his assurance of his trust in certain fixed
principles, which could not be wholly proved
by an outward demonstration, but of which
he was confident through his inner conviction or intuition or valid feeling, that he
quoted with approval a small girl whose pro-
test he had heard on a noisy Boston street.
The child had made her statement of what
she believed a fact. Her companions had
challenged her. They jeered, they laughed.
But she stood her ground for the truth as
she saw it, exclaiming, "I don't keer—and I
don't keer if I don't keer." What was lack
of earthly approval, if one had conviction
like that!

After this I saw Dr. Royce only occasion-
a'ly, at the meetings of a philosophical club,
or upon the street. One Sunday afternoon
I met him on a Cambridge street car. He
looked tired. I asked him where he had
been, for he was carrying a large travelling
bag. "Oh," he said demurely, "I've been
in New York. I've been giving lectures on

philosophy to a woman's club in New York every Saturday afternoon. The first lecture was a respectable philosophical lecture, but I saw that they didn't understand a word of it. So since then I've been giving them 'guff' —and they think philosophy's great." We laughed, and at Harvard Square we parted. I think I never saw him again.

But I continued to be his pupil. Living far away, unable to see him, I planned to read his books as he sent them forth. So I came under his spell as he declared his inspiring Doctrine of Loyalty. It was to be his theme to the end with enlargements and variations. To those who put high value on the Church, his words about loyalty to the Beloved Community, were as a fresh revelation. I was moved by his *Sources of Religious Insight*. Perhaps the profoundest note in this book is the passage about finding God in the depths. We come, he said, to such deep places that we can only cry. We are astonished that we can cry.

And then we become aware that our cry is
heard. And He who hears is God. And
so, he continued, God is often defined for the
plain man as He who hears men's cry from
the depths. One has no right to see in public
utterance the revelation of a writer's personal experience, but I have always wondered if this great confession of God's presence were not the outcome of his own sorrow
in the death of his only son. If so it was
a demonstration of his own doctrine, which
I had learned in his class-room years before,
that truth is not only that which can be
described, but also that which can be only
appreciated by experience.

His two volumes on Christianity struck
again the notes of loyalty, especially loyalty
to the Beloved Community. The part which
most appealed to me was the section on Sacrifice and Atonement. Before there was a
world war to teach us, he revealed the eternal
truth in the doctrine of vicarious sacrifice
and in atonement. Even the Church had

grown silent, or at times had tried to explain the doctrine away. He made it plain even to the man who felt no obligation to ancient formularies. The lack of the book is that it makes Christ into a Beloved Community, and says nothing of the loyalty which the saints have delighted to give to Christ Himself—their enthusiasm, their devotion, their love to a personal Leader and Master.

Apart from books Dr. Royce was a living example of loyalty. When his dearest friend, William James, became a pragmatist, Royce like another St. Paul dealing with St. Peter, "withstood him to the face." There was for Royce an absolute Ideal, eternal in the heavens; and our fluctuating understandings and needs could not change it. He was also perplexed by Professor James's sympathetic attention to mediums. There was a tale, very likely apocryphal, that when the famous Spanish medium, who had won James's approval of her genuineness, was afterwards caught in a palpable fraud, Royce sent to James the following lines:

> Eny, meney, miney, mo:
> Catch Eusapia by the toe.
> If she hollers, that will show,
> James's theories are not so!

Of course the philosophical difference served only to make the friendship stronger.

The most vivid instance of his loyalty came towards the end. When the European War began he tried to stand aside in philosophic detachment. But as it was borne in upon him what Germany was trying to do and was doing, he boldly fled from his neutrality, and in public speech and in published articles declared his allegiance to the Cause of England and France and their Allies. He did not live to see his own country striving in the high cause for truth and righteousness; but it may be that his ringing words hastened the day of our entering the strife. Once more he demonstrated that philosophy is practical and is from life to richer life. Possibly his own death was hastened by the intensity of his plea: he may have been part of the vicarious sacrifice by which the man who loves righteousness loves it so completely that he lays down his life for his friends.

I am an orthodox person. I suppose Josiah Royce felt neither the fetters nor the inspiration of orthodoxy. But he was a deeply religious man, bent upon finding God and serving Him with all his mind and heart and strength. He took me out of the closed rooms which religion sometimes cherishes; and, quite in the open spaces, led me to gaze into the sky and far away to the melting horizon, and to be unafraid. I want thus late to speak my gratitude.

ALEXANDER VIETS
GRISWOLD ALLEN

ALEXANDER VIETS GRISWOLD ALLEN

SOON after I entered Harvard College I began to know by sight Dr. Alexander Viets Griswold Allen, Professor of Church History in the Episcopal Theological School on Brattle Street. Only when I entered his classes five years later did I come to know him. Meantime I was from time to time meeting his enthusiastic pupils; and once he gave to the college students a public evening lecture on Reading, which I heard. This lecture was my first real introduction to the unique qualities of this truly great teacher. He related to us, in his low musical voice, his own first adventures as a reader. He described the little Western College where he began to browse among the books of the college library. A yellow-covered magazine attracted him. It was the Westminster Review. To the timid New England lad from a country rectory its radicalism was amazing and thrilling. It introduced him to Mill and Carlyle, to Coleridge and F. D. Maurice— he thereupon read everything the library contained of them. And so the voyages upon unknown seas were begun. He made his speeches, studied his lessons, and deepened his friendships, but the real romance of his college life was this learning the joy of reading for its own sake.

Here, evidently was no conventional theological professor. On the whole, even on that night, I recognized that he was more of a humanist than any man I had known. I had known distinguished masters who had taught me Greek and Latin and English and philosophy, men of real learning and brilliant power; but none of them seemed to

give quite this same human sympathy for
the genius of the past. The German
philologist was still binding the consciences
of teachers of literature; and history was
over-worried lest it get a fact out of place,
with never a thought of its meaning in any
case. Here was a man who someway escaped
the dragon. I awaited the day when I might
call myself his pupil.

When that day came, I found him more
than a humanist, though he never ceased to
be a humanist. As he guided us through
the mazes of Church History, he was revealed a prophet. For history ceased to be
a series of accidents, human achievements,
and human failures; it became, under his
touch, the manifest expression of God's
leadership in human affairs. He strengthened our faith. He did for us, in a small
group, what Phillips Brooks was doing for
the multitude. Both were prophets of the
Most High.

Besides lectures four mornings a week, he

held for us seminars once a fortnight. We all looked forward to both lectures and seminars as the chief pleasure and stimulus of our scholastic life. We all averred, though we might formerly have sat under James, or Norton, or Shaler, that we had never known such a teacher. Dean Gray was wont to say, laughing, that it was no use to have chairs of Theology, New Testament, etc., for Allen taught them all. And the jest was the truth; such is the privilege of the man who teaches ecclesiastical history. When we studied the Apostolic and sub-Apostolic age he warned us that the only safe commentary of the New Testament is Church History: he saw the mistake which German-taught theologians were making in limiting the New Testament to itself and disregarding its subsequent historical context. When he reached Athanasius and the Council of Nicæa, we found his living picture of the Council not a whit more absorbing than his intricate and subtle exposition of the doctrine of the Trinity. That and similar doctrines of the Faith were to him no cold external formulæ, but had fused themselves into his experience: he spoke of them with the hushed enthusiasm with which Dante might have spoken of Beatrice.

No doubt, too, much of Dr. Allen's indefinable charm came from his voice. The stranger who heard him in a large church or in a public hall was inevitably disappointed. "I couldn't hear him," was the constant complaint of such a stranger. He himself was conscious that he was not reaching his audience or congregation, and the thought bound him with chains: he could not get what he called his freedom. In the lecture-room—just large enough for twenty students, more or less—he was as free as the April wind. He brought into the lecture-room a number of books, perhaps a note-book; but he seldom looked at anything except the faces of his pupils. He once confessed that if he saw an intelligent man losing interest he instantly changed his tack. His voice, as resonant as a violin, was not merely naturally beautiful; it was in some way tuned to the minds of his men. It was pleading, all unconsciously, for the truth. His sensitiveness, concealed ordinarily, vibrated through his whole being. He was perpetually adjusting his message to the understanding of the young men for whom he felt a loving responsibility.

Had his appeal been only one of charm, we should not have called him the master we found him to be. With the charm, the consideration, the courtesy, was bound up a startling virility. His reproof, his mockery, his just irony, were sometimes so gently expressed that the man did not at once awake to their biting austerity. But when he afterwards let the words into his mind he was stung with their sharpness. A man once said to him, with patronizing condescension, that he hadn't yet decided whether he should come to his special seminar on F. D. Maurice.

Dr. Allen, smiling sweetly, said with a finality not to be mistaken, "Don't you think it
would be better to wait till you are asked?"

Perhaps we learned to know him better in
the seminars than in the lecture-room. The
evening was spent in listening to three
papers read by the men. After the reading,
Dr. Allen made his comments. First, we
exulted in his appreciation. He saw many
high lights: we thought him unduly indul-
gent when he saw promise in a neighbour;
but our hearts beat fast when he saw hopeful
things in ourselves. He was alert to detect
any note of perception or originality. He
also fell upon any unfortunate sentence
which seemed to him unreal or cheap. Once
after an exhibition of priggish niceness in a
paper he said apropos of nothing at all,
"Uneducated people use bad grammar; half-
educated people use good grammar; really
cultivated people use any grammar they
please." He would follow an excessively
modern paper with the remark, "Well, to

leave this so-called nineteenth century for a moment——;" or, "Humanly speaking— as they say in Brooklyn——" And then he would go on to talk of a great personality, or a wide flung movement in history, or a fundamental doctrine, bringing to bear his knowledge and experience, his sympathy and his humour, his reverence, his adoration. Sometimes we went to our rooms as if we had been present at some searching and inspiring service. Our hearts had been lifted up.

By a happy accident, I broke through my shyness and began to call upon him in his study. Later I elected to write the thesis for my bachelor's degree in his department, and that gave me excuse to see him some- what oftener. And what hours those were when he gave one his best! It seemed a selfish sin to be the only listener. But as the seminar showed a new aspect of his genius, richer than that shown in his lectures; so his private counsel still seems to me to

ALEXANDER VIETS GRISWOLD ALLEN IN HIS STUDY.

have excelled both lecture and seminar. He too was shy. He had deep reserves. Sometimes he let himself go, and told the secret enthusiasms and hopes and fears of life, as he could not have told them to more than one person at a time. I don't know how many sought him one by one. I suppose a good many ventured.

Till he died his letters followed me in my wanderings. He never failed to speak of my work, to show that he cared, to urge me to keep up my reading and study in the rather active ministries which fell to my lot. He told me of distinguished foreigners who happened to come to Cambridge. He told me their foibles and limitations, their contribution and their exceptional values. He commented on the books he was reading; he told me what he was writing. There never was a master who kept a distant pupil so patiently by his side. It was the glory of a month to have a letter come from him. Everything went better for it—preaching, study, pastoral responsibility, joy in one's lot.

Once in two or three years I would drop in upon him for an afternoon, as I prowled about upon a seaboard holiday. He was apt still to be in Cambridge, bent upon using the summer desert (which Cambridge always becomes when the University closes) for some uninterrupted writing. Now it was *Christian Institutions,* again it was the *Life of Phillips Brooks.* He took one into his confidence and showed the method of his work. The mystical sense was always with him. He would confess that he hadn't intended a book to be what it was evidently developing to be; but, he said, we must put aside our plans and do what we are led to do. His reverence for Christ was paramount; after that he had a consuming reverence for all human personality. It is the defect and also the power of his memoir of Brooks that in this task he deliberately stilled his critical faculty. When he knew so much as he knew

of Brooks, through all the revelations of letters and journals and sermons, as well as
through his own friendship, he could not
descend to petty analysis. It was like trying
to discover, as one reader did try to discover,
the size of Brooks's hat, and the length of
his shoes. Dr. Allen took his hero whole.

One of the amusing symbols which he kept
about him in his characteristic study—which
was uncommonly filled with personality—
was a double cartoon of Gladstone and
Disraeli. "Yes," he would say as a visitor
laughed at the two pictures, "there he stands
talking—the country's William—guarding
the treasure-chest; and Dizzy sits ineffably
bored." The strange relationship of these
two men always touched his humour. When
Gladstone's *Life* came out, he read it dili-
gently, though not increasing thereby his
admiration for the G. O. M., which, to tell
the truth, was never exalted. On one of
my visits he was full of the man and the
period. He said that it came over him on

a certain afternoon that he would like to hear the great man's voice; so he went into Boston, and, dropping into a phonographic shop, asked the shopkeeper if he had a record of the voice of Gladstone. He did have; and obligingly invited Dr. Allen to listen to it. It was exceedingly dim and muffled. The shopkeeper, seeing Dr. Allen's disappointment, said reassuringly, "We have a record here which is very fine, and I am sure you will like that much better: it is a record of the voice of T. Dewitt Talmage." Dr. Allen thanked him, and listened, with an inward chuckle, as the stentorian tones rolled and rumbled. It rather pleased him that the shopkeeper thought that he was the sort of person who would be glad to hear Dr. Talmage.

Sometimes my summer visit came soon after a long journey. Perhaps he had spent a summer in Scotland; then he would have amusing flings at the shovel-hats of ecclesiastical Edinburgh. "These Scotch parsons must be wonderfully good," he would say, "to transcend the depressing effect of their hats." Or he would tell of the Scotch kirk where he heard the preacher define the obligations of the Sabbath. "The congregation," he said, "the whole fifteen hundred of them, sat like a jury in a box to see that no heresy was spoken."

Of all my summer visits to him, I think the most exciting was the first I chanced to make after his winter in Rome. He found in it all the history which he had been studying for forty years. He followed clues. He confirmed old theories, and made discoveries. His imagination made him live in the Rome of St. Paul, of Hildebrand, of Leo X. Moreover he found congenial friends in Rome to whom he could pour out his soul. Perhaps the most interesting was the daughter of the historian Froude. And all the time he was writing letters home which intimately recorded the high experience of a lifetime. A deep sorrow came that winter, and the history took upon itself the tragedy as well ·as the confidence. He wrote of a childlike faith. Through all illusions and disillusions, he trusted the Saviour and His promise.

The last letter I had from him was written just before he died. He told me that in his delirium he had said to the night nurse that he wanted me to edit something of Origen's which his dream warned him had just been discovered. It was like him to trust an old pupil, believing that the pupil could do a task which he himself would have liked to undertake. He had been asked by the School Trustees to sit for his portrait; but he was too ill for that. In a way, this illness came as a blessing in relieving him of the embarrassment of "posing." "Besides," he said, "neither Plotinus nor Dr. Pusey would sit for his portrait. Why should I?"

When he had gone, many a man lost not only a master but a dear friend. He believed in men, who were neither very good nor very clever; his generous belief kept them humble, rather than puffed them up. He gave them confidence in their task. And he left them always at the feet of the one Master, whom to serve was his own joy and freedom.

HENRY SYLVESTER NASH

HENRY SYLVESTER NASH

FOR forty years Henry Sylvester Nash was one of the most familiar figures on the streets of the American Cambridge. As an undergraduate at Harvard he was known as the man who had taken out of the college library more books than any other man who had lived in Cambridge. To most people he was the man whose face was uncompromisingly "plain," perhaps the "plainest" they had ever seen; yet this face was so compellingly attractive that one instinctively turned to ask, "Who is that man?" When a Boston clergyman heard the theological student tell with bated breath what Dr. Nash meant to him, the city rector was inclined to smile over the enthusiasm of youth; till he himself, at some club or service, heard Nash in one of his exalted moods, when the Spirit, using his knowledge and training, declared, through a countenance transfigured, the word of the Lord—and then the city rector too spoke of Nash with a catch in his voice. For many years Dr. Nash's followers were confined to his small classes in the Theological School in Cambridge, and to the little congregation to whom he ministered on Sundays at Chestnut Hill. It was only later that the larger world discovered him.

He was accustomed to have men under him who came with thorough university training. He therefore assumed capacity and willingness to work hard. When I was his pupil, he spent the first year in a rapid reading of the Greek Testament, with introductions to the various books, and special consideration of the Synoptic problem and the sources of the Life of Christ; the second year, we worked over the Epistle to the Romans in minute detail; the third year was

devoted to the Fourth Gospel. I remember
how in the first year he threw us up against
the most difficult critical questions of the
age. We wrote nine theses that first year.
The first was on the Tübingen Hypothesis
—of which till then none of us had ever
heard. We then wrote a thesis based upon
a reading of the New Testament to find
every reference and allusion to the Parousia:
these references and allusions we tabulated
and arranged, that he might have, from first-
hand knowledge, the New Testament doctrine. He commanded us to read many
"Lives" of Christ—which he designated—
and required us to relate in a thesis the point
of view and method of each. Some men
were frightened by the robustness of his
attack. His was no Sunday-school course,
shielding our faith. We were given the
supreme documents of Christianity and we
were set to find their meaning and their
truth. If they were filled with hard questions which might later unsettle our faith,

we were forced to face the issue at once,
while we were yet only candidates for the
Ministry. Dr. Nash treated us on the first
day of his course as grown men who must
know all.

It is only fair to say, however, that in
meeting whatever difficulties there were, we
had the superb help of Dr. Nash's own faith.
He never dodged the perplexities. Some
critical questions he felt to be settled. Others
he held in solution. Still others he believed
insoluble in this world. Once when a pupil
asked him what St. Paul meant by a certain
phrase, he said with a reverence which was
from the heart, "I don't know: that is one
of the questions I mean to ask St. Paul when
I see him." Nash was at his height in his
exposition of the Epistle to the Romans. He
struggled to give us all that commentators
in the past had thought of this passage and
that; then, with this historic interpretation
fused with his own best thought, he gave us
his interpretation; and, beyond that, he gave

Painted by Wilton Lockwood.

HENRY SYLVESTER NASH.

us the profound expression of his own faith.
Then it was that we would look up from
our note books—in which we had been writing furiously to get every word down—to
discover that the face of our dear teacher,
once thought exceedingly plain, was radi-
antly beautiful, shining as the face of an
angel. We knew that the Holy Ghost was
upon him.

He had an exasperatingly difficult style.
He used technical language: this was easily
acquired, and we soon learned his vocabulary.
But he used also a language which was no
one's but his own. It was hard to follow.
Even the illustrations—which were apt to be
very odd indeed, sometimes grotesque—were
mystifying. Pupils and others sometimes
thought this strange style an affectation. But
it was not. He regretted it, and tried with
all his might to acquire a simpler vehicle for
his thought. To a certain extent he succeeded. But only measurably. His books
fail to have the readers they deserve, be-

cause even an intelligent and eager reader is baffled. It was in his preaching, finally, that he escaped almost wholly: and those who heard him at his best must always think of him as one of the great preachers of the Church; for he brought one up to the high places of thought and feeling.

After I had been in the Ministry several years, he published his first book, *The Genesis of the Social Conscience*. He had written me that it was coming out, and I longed to see it. I felt that at last the world at large was to know him somewhat as his pupils knew him. But it was discouragingly hard reading, as everyone knows who has attempted it; I knew that not many would have patience to dig for the genuine gold within it. I saw instantly that it was a great book: It stirred me to write sermon after sermon; and it must awaken every reader to expression and action. I trust that this book may live to inspire seekers for the truth through the years.

When Dr. Nash spoke at a Church Congress, it was commonly reported that his was the high word of the Congress. He struck the spiritual note, and fire flashed from it. Not long before he died he was invited to New York to speak, along with Dr. McGiffert, at a meeting of clergymen. The subject was the Life of Christ. Dr. McGiffert spoke with the clear incisiveness of the critical scholar. He told the somewhat cold details of modern research. Then Dr. Nash rose. He had not come with a definite speech in mind. But at all times full of the subject, he broke in where Dr. McGiffert had dropped it, and went forward with the positive findings. To the same technical equipment which Dr. McGiffert had, he added the prophet's insight, and he spoke out of heart, as well as mind, his loyalty to his Master. Now and again I meet a man who asks me if I remember Nash on that day.

Preëminently a theologian, he reached out

into the abounding life which surrounded him. Always delicate and frail, one of his chief enthusiasms was foot-ball: he called it the most spiritual of games, and he watched it with the same devout interest with which he studied a new book. He was an intense patriot. The School suspended lectures on national days; and he always urged his men to read American biography on these holidays. He was religiously democratic. The son of a poor clergyman, he was himself poor all his days. Someway we could not have imagined him rich. He longed to be at one with all the brethren of Christ. He would sometimes remind us that we ought not to shrink from the thought that our Lord was accustomed to be with the sort of people who in our time eat with their knives. If He did not shrink, neither must we. He had a beautiful chivalry in the presence of servants. Without departing from any conventionality he would by a glance, a smile, or the slightest of words, acknowledge even

at another's table the acts of service by which
he was surrounded. I had to watch him
somewhat narrowly to discover these tokens
of brotherhood; but, so far as I could see,
they were always there. They never approached the familiar: they were stately,
simple, the inherent expression of a real
reverence for all who serve. He was a great
gentleman, who made many other gentlemen
look quite cheap, because their consideration
and courtesy stopped short, in that they had
not sufficient imagination, wit, and courage
to make their kindness universal.

His family was his joy. "Our children,"
he wrote me one Summer, "are teaching us
things and things." A man told me, first
with laughter and then with tears, that he
had seen Dr. Nash bringing his children
home late one evening in a street-car from
some excursion. The children were weary,
and the youngest was inclined to weep. This
youngest sat on his father's knee while Nash
jumped him up and down, singing snatches

of "Ta-ra-ra-ra-boom-de-ay," absolutely un-conscious of the smiling car-full of people.

He drew from an inexhaustible reservoir of love within his soul which, lavished first upon his own, he gave with only less fervour to his pupils. He watched over us. He wrote us letters of affection, however far we wandered. He reminded us that every day he remembered us in the Chapel. The Chapel, for him was filled with the men whom he had taught, whom he loved, and for whom he never forgot to pray.

The last time he stayed under my roof I asked him what we could do to stop a certain unhappy tale which was likely to make a friend first miserable and then useless. Neither of us believed it. "I heard the story," he confessed; "but I locked it up in my memory and never have even referred to it." And then he went on to speak of sin. "I have the greatest sympathy," he said, "with a man who is even justly accused of such a crime. I think how easy it would

be for me to do the same thing." I knew
that he couldn't have done it for all the
world; but I knew that I had one more proof
of his saintship, in that he cried always, "God
be merciful to me, a sinner."

Tender, compassionate as he was, he had
his fine contempt. I think he despised most
of all the people who were always thrusting
themselves forward into the limelight, to
strut up and down with their insufficient
wares. He gave them ridiculous nicknames,
and laughed at all their tawdry display. In
contrast with this, he never considered the
size of his audience when he uttered his
prophecy. One day a woman came to ask
me if there could not be an opportunity made
to have Dr. Nash give to considerable numbers certain expositions of the Faith which
she and one other woman had heard. She
said that, living for the Summer hard by
Dr. Nash's Summer home, they had gone to
ask his help in certain intellectual difficulties.
Whereupon he asked them to come to him

at convenient hours and he would talk to
them. "Then," she said, "for us two lone
women he gave what were more than any
lectures or sermons we had ever heard. He
re-created our faith. We felt wicked to be
the only people who heard him. But he went
on talking as if he had had thousands before
him." It was part of his religion to give
his best without thought of numbers and applause. Any other consideration would have
seemed to him, to say the least, unspeakably
vulgar.

His fidelity to the Theological School in
Cambridge was one of his outstanding char-
acteristics. A larger income would have
been acceptable for the sake of those whom
he loved better than his own life. Large
parishes held out welcoming hands; a diocese
filled with his warm friends was, through
them, informally offered him. But he did
not for a moment consider what some men
might have called a wider field. He spoke
impersonally of the folly of the teacher at-

tempting to be a pastor: a man, he said, must
do the thing for which all his life long he
has been trained. But we who had heard
him preach, and we who had known his
shepherding of our own souls, knew how the
affection of either parish or diocese would
have kindled in his loving presence. The real
reason was deeper: he could not help knowing what he was to the School. He had been
its servant from the opening of his Ministry;
he would be its servant to the end. He could
not leave it.

In the crowded Chapel where he had
prayed day after day we gathered to praise
God for his life, finished in its earthly stage.
There were the tokens of death. But it was
given us to transcend them. He was glori-
ously alive, and we knew it. The Light
which we had seen upon his face had received
him into everlasting habitations, and he was
at home.

BISHOP WHIPPLE

BISHOP WHIPPLE

I CANNOT remember when I did not know Bishop Whipple's name. Through my boyhood I thought of him as the great friend of the Indians, working for them in Minnesota, pleading for them in Washington, a patriot of the sort Washington would have liked, a primitive patriot who had survived into our own time. As I learned more of him, he seemed, rather, like St. John: for in the reports of his words there was the same insistence upon the primacy of love. This double judgment may have been keener than I suspected. For the Bishop in his early manhood had dipped into political life; and his experience with men of all sorts stood him in good stead in his later missionary labours, when he combined the wisdom of the serpent with the gentleness of the dove. One of his old friends used to say, "Bishop Whipple is ninety-nine parts St. John, and one part New York politician."

At last I saw this interesting man face to face. He had come to Boston to act as one of the presenters at Bishop Brooks's consecration; and in calling upon an old rector in an hotel, I found myself being presented to Bishop Whipple. He was gaunt, tall, with long hair, with a patriarchal face. (I think Henry Irving must have learned from Bishop Whipple how to walk as Becket.) He passed from one to another, saying his word of affection to this old friend or that; and his voice could not be forgotten. In his youth, I have been told, this voice had a marvellous resonance and appeal: to the end, though diminished, it was such a voice as would awaken a man's thought of the open fields and the wide skies.

A number of years passed, and I became

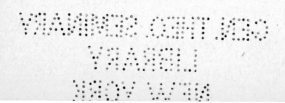

Bishop Whipple's neighbour, in the Minnesota community which for more than forty years was his home. When I began my work there, he was away, and for several months I could see how, even in his absence, his spirit dominated everything in the town. It was not only that people were proud of him: they looked up to him as to a father, and all seemed to have some personal association with him. If he had not confirmed them, he had said a kind word in some great sorrow, or he had preached a sermon which helped, or one had years before worked on his Cathedral, and each Saturday night the Bishop had paid him with the rest. The Church schools as well as the Cathedral had been built up through his energy and persuasiveness. One of the chief benefactors of the boys' school had said, "I will not see that old man." But he was not old, and she some way did see him; and afterwards she reported, "When he had talked about his work for half an hour, I was ready to give him

every penny I had." The Chicago fire followed hard upon the pledges she made, but
from the burning city she telegraphed to the
Bishop that he should have the buildings she
had promised if they took all she had left.
Such stories the people told of their Bishop;
and awaited his home-coming as they would
have awaited a beloved member of their own
families.

His sermons always had the spirit of his
patriotism and the spirit of his devotion to
the Indians. He nearly always made some
reference to our earlier generals or statesmen, and one could be sure to hear of "our
dear red brothers of the forest." There were
certain recurring phrases. He would speak
of the Holy Communion as "the trysting-
place of love." Or he would mention some
colleague as one who "gave him love un-
clouded by a doubt." Making much of
earnest Christian people not of our Communion, he pleaded constantly for Christian
Unity.

To know Bishop Whipple in his most characteristic leadership one must have seen him among his Indians. When his diocese was divided, few Indians were left under his direct care; but he would go at least once a year to Birch Coulee. On Saturday night he would gather the Dakotas about him for religious instruction, as preparation for Baptism and Confirmation the next day. He spoke to them as to children, in homely, practical words which not one of them could fail to understand. Because they told him all their hopes and troubles, he knew their sorrows and temptations. He was their great chief, and they loved him as only children can love a father.

I was set one day to examine a solitary Indian for Deacons' Orders. If the Bishop loved white men, there was no word strong enough to tell his devotion to the Indians. On this particular day he did not intend to leave the fate of his beloved Indian to any chance. He met me in the hall, warning me that the candidate had been dispensed from Greek. I said that I remembered. "And remember," added the Bishop, "that he is an Indian. You must ask the questions simply." I gave my promise. Even so, the Bishop thought it well to accompany me, and sat close beside me as I put my questions. I was encouragingly inquisitive at first, asking how many Gospels there were, who wrote the Epistles to the Corinthians, and after a few more such questions, I said, "How does the Epistle of St. James differ from the other Epistles in the New Testament?" A look of dismay came over the face of the handsome Indian. Without looking at the Bishop, I could feel that he was growing uncomfortable. After a long silence he leaned over to me and said: "You don't quite know how to put questions to an Indian. Do you mind if I ask him?" Of course, I begged him to put the question. Whereupon, with a radiant smile, which told the would-be deacon that help was coming, the Bishop said assuringly: "Now, John, St. James doesn't tell you what you ought to think; he tells you what you ought to do. Now, doesn't he, John?" After a moment's hesitation, with fine Indian dignity, there came the slow reply, "Yes, Sir." "You see," whispered the Bishop to me, with a look of triumph, "he understands perfectly." Is it wonderful that the Indians, and all others who knew him, loved him? He was perpetually coming to our help.

On another morning I was summoned to the Bishop's study to examine some white candidates for the ministry. We sat in the pleasant room lined with books, many of which were presentation copies from men like Lightfoot and Westcott. Hardly any set of books was complete, because he had a way of urging students and clergy to borrow what they liked—and alas! many books went out never to return. Pictures of his friends in England and America were everywhere. Bits of Indian bead-work were hanging over chairs and screens. The room could have belonged to no one but Bishop Whipple. Well, there we sat, and the young candidates refused to be frightened in so genial an atmosphere. At length one was so far from worried about his attainments that he sallied forth to examine the Bishop. "Bishop," he began, "Bishop Tuttle has lent one of our churches in St. Louis to the Presbyterians for their services, because their church has burned down. What do you think of that, Sir?" Bishop Whipple slipped still farther down into his big chair, and looking out into the leaves of the June maples, said, "I have all I can do, taking care of you youngsters: I leave Bishop Tuttle to take care of his own diocese." There were no more diversions.

The more strenuous days of Bishop Whipple were over when I knew him. His son once told me something of the rigours of the early days, when the Bishop on his visitations would sleep in winter bedrooms which

Bishop Whipple.

were not only cold as only Minnesota can be cold, but had perhaps not been open since the previous May. Once this son went with his father, and they were assigned to the same room; naturally he began to make the usual preparations for bed. The Bishop noticed him. "Charlie, Charlie," he said nervously, "what are you doing? Keep your clothes on; keep your coat on; keep your hat on—keep everything on. Get into bed just as you are!" The Bishop never got colds through indiscretion. In spite of incessant travelling, he never ceased to fear that he would lose a train. He must have spent in railway stations what would make an ordinary lifetime. His sister-in-law said to him one day, as he was urging Mrs. Whipple to start with him for the train long before the time: "Brother Henry, why do you want to go now? You know she never loses a train." "I know it," he said in despair, "that's the worst of it." He was quite as eager to begin a service. He was always

sitting in the robing-room fifteen or twenty
minutes before the hour appointed, turning
to the rector every moment or two with the
cheerful question, "Now, my dear brother,
it's time to begin; isn't it?" One had to keep
telling him that the congregation hadn't
come, then that the choristers hadn't all
come, then that the bell hadn't rung—and
at last it was a wise rector who hid himself
till the right moment was reached.

He was one of the most generous of men.
I remember that one morning he gave me
a surplice which he thought would be convenient for a visiting clergyman. In the
afternoon he sent me a note, asking me if
I wouldn't give it back; for a missionary had
dropped in, who, he was sure, needed it more
than the imaginary visitor. I remember, too,
what a difficult task it was to give out
church notices if I was near him in the
chancel: he kept up a rapid series of whispered suggestions as I was talking, "Now, my
brother, tell them this; now, my brother, tell

them that." He wanted all possible invitations to be given them!

This childlike love is what one remembers most in thinking of him. He was pleased and grateful for any word of appreciation. He had so much adulation from the great of the earth that we felt that he did not care for our poor words at home. But he did care deeply. He had letters of frank affection from one Archbishop of Canterbury after another, or, for example, from Mr. Gladstone; he knew nearly all the leaders of his generation in the English-speaking world. He had Mr. Gladstone's walking-stick, which was the great man's parting gift to him on his last visit. When he returned from a Lambeth Conference with a new degree from Oxford, he put on his beautiful doctor's gown, at Mrs. Whipple's request, to show it to his sister-in-law, who was also his very old friend. When he turned about, Mrs. George Whipple said, "Oh, Brother Henry, don't you feel grand!" "Oh,

Sister Mary," said he, "you do say such uncomfortable things." "Well," she answered, "I don't want to spoil you." At which he winked, and said, "That's a sin, Sister Mary, that will never be laid at your door." Being Scotch, she liked the compliment.

He was in truth fond of colour. When he returned to us after a long absence, he was wont to invite his friends and neighbours to his house. I remember, before one such reception, he came downstairs with his usual elegance of appearance, winning the evident admiration of his family, till they looked at his feet, and there they saw, above his shining low shoes, the most brilliant of red stockings. The ladies instantly decided that he must change them. He was crestfallen, but obediently withdrew. In a few moments, as the first guests came, he entered, altogether in black; but there was a gleam in his eye, and, as he passed me, he whispered, "I have on a pink undershirt, anyway."

Days and months went by. His young Coadjutor died, and he did more work in his diocese than he had done for many years. Almost eighty, he seemed to have the strength of a young man. He was used to thinking himself ill when the doctor thought him fairly well; and he would refuse to leave his bed, till suddenly it occurred to him that he must keep a distant engagement, and from bed he went upon long journeys, evidently none the worse. When his pocket-book was stolen from him he said, "I don't mind the loss of the money, but I do mind losing those excellent prescriptions; I think I had twenty in that pocketbook!" We laughed, and felt confident that the elastic constitution which had borne him through many vicissitudes would bear him far into old age—especially since he was daily guarded by a wise and watchful love.

But the end was sudden, one September night after a brief illness. I was with him all that night. Indians came from the

Dakotas and the Chippewas to speak their last loving farewells in the familiar house where his body lay. Men strong and good whom he had known from childhood bore his body to the Cathedral, and throngs of people within and without gave thanks for all that he had been to them and to countless others. I never heard, "Jesus, Lover of My Soul" sung as I heard it sung that afternoon to old St. Martin's. Then the Dakotas sang a hymn in their own tongue within the church, and the Chippewas sang a hymn in their language outside the church. When the people with bowed heads were moving towards their homes, one of the bishops who had officiated said, "You buried your Bishop like a prince." We hoped we had; for he was more than a prince: he was a dear friend and counsellor, a most loving father.

TWO COUSINS BY MARRIAGE

TWO COUSINS BY MARRIAGE

THERE is a peculiar interest in two faces on a single canvas. The suggestion of influence, comradeship, and love makes each face gain from the other. For no sensible painter would dare to paint two faces on a canvas without intimating by a glance or the touch of the hand that each was conscious of the other. So I am going to try to sketch the characters of two unusual women whom I knew in a Minnesota town long ago.

One of these was Mrs. George Whipple, the sister-in-law of Bishop Whipple. She had come to Minnesota with her sister, Mrs. James Lloyd Breck. When Bishop Whipple came to Minnesota, his brother promptly fell in love with Miss Mary Mills; so one of the happiest homes ever seen or written about came into being.

When I knew Mrs. Whipple, Mr. Whipple had been long dead, but I served a parish of which he had been rector many years before, and Mrs. Whipple gave me an instant friendship, which deepened with the years. Through her I learned to know the unselfish and whimsical man whose memory was lovingly cherished by all the people who had known him. She told me how she was forced to lock up her clothes; because, whenever poor people came his way, he gave, first, all his own things, then all hers, so far as he could lay hold of them. To hear her tell the tale you would have thought that she was a flinty person dismally resenting the indiscriminate giving; but no wife could ever have more eagerly aided and abetted the criminal generosity. An old friend in making a call never dared to admire a possession, new or old, lest at the first favourable oppor-

tunity it come to his doorstep, with an irre-
sistible note.

She was full of anecdote. She and Mr.
Whipple had lived for a considerable time
as missionaries in the Hawaiian Islands. She
never tired of telling stories of "T. Nettle-
ship Honolulu" (this was Bishop Staley),
Bishop Willis, and the other English;
Queen Emma, and the other natives; all of
whom made life in the sunny islands diverting. She and her Philadelphia friend, Miss
Darlington (together, of course, with Bishop
and Mrs. Whipple), had everything to do
with the early traditions of St. Mary's Hall,
a school for girls founded in Bishop Whipple's own home. Of her brothers-in-law, Dr.
Breck and Bishop Whipple, and their blithe
and heroic days of laying foundations in
Minnesota, she had the liveliest recollections.
In the vine-covered stone cottage where a
large part of her life was spent, clergymen,
daughters of St. Mary's, and many others
came from afar to see her, not from sense

of duty, but for the vivacious and illuminating talk which they knew they certainly would hear there.

She at one time edited the diocesan newspaper, and I suppose it was never so good as when her racy pen told the news of Bishop Whipple and his band of friendly missionaries. She never allowed herself to grow rusty in the literature or the harder knowledge which made the background of her culture. She was quite likely to decide that she would read again, for example, all the Waverley novels—and do it. When she could not sleep, she told me, she would light her lamp and in the night watches do intricate problems in some branch of mathematics. Such were her pastimes when she was slipping past her eightieth year.

With her strong Scotch face, framed in her ample widow's cap, she seemed, to those who did not know her well, rather austere. The silly and the worldly stood in awe of her for their good. And the man or the

MARY JOANNA WHIPPLE.

woman who hesitated in decisions, when the right was plain, understood her scorn. In a scholastic house which had once been her home, a portrait belonging to the house was missing. When its absence caused pain to people who she knew should not be troubled, Mrs. Whipple at some inconvenience made a friendly call, and standing before the wall where the portrait had hung, said sternly, "What has become of the portrait which always hung here?" "Ah," said the master of the house nervously, "it is in the attic: ah, ah, the ladies—you know the ladies always have their way." Mrs. Whipple drew herself up. "Not in *my* house," she said. She was wont to tell the story with glee; and never probably knew just why we laughed so hard. I remember one encounter which I had in connection with portraits. In a hall in memory of Mr. Whipple we were collecting portraits of those who had contributed loyal service to the community. One day she looked at me in silence with a piercing gaze, as if she would read just how far this collecting of portraits might go. Then she said suddenly with a finality not to be mistaken, "If you ever put a picture of me there after I am gone—well, I'll come back and—and visit you!"

This austerity was the thin disguise over one of the tenderest hearts God ever made. She planned happiness for those who were not happy. She saved out of her meagre income a proportion which a princess might envy, that great causes might have the utmost she could spare. Having no children, she adopted two little girls who gave her love for love; one died as a child, the other in the maturity of a brilliant womanhood. Then younger women gave her the devotion which daughters might have shown, and she was not alone. Moreover her love went out to the dumb beasts. When a neighbour kept a young dog in a box and (according to Mrs. Whipple's observant eye) forgot to feed it for days at a time, Mrs. Whipple would

wander aimlessly in the early morning—
hours before the neighbours' curtains were
drawn—and give the poor beast food and
water for the day. The cats and dogs
knew her susceptibilities, and when deserted
would come, dilapidated and forlorn, to her
porch. In they were brought, tended, and
fed as babies in a nursery. If no owner
appeared, they were given later, sleek and
fat, to boys and girls who were thought to
deserve them, and who would surely be kind.
She always had a permanent cat and a
permanent dog. The dog I chanced to know
was Mungo—a wiry, scraggy being, with
snapping eyes and with the whirl of a
Dervish when he was glad. He ordinarily
accompanied his mistress on her walks and
drives. I remember, one morning, she said,
"Now, Mungo, be a good dog; I am going
to church—you must stay at home." "But,
Mrs. Whipple," I protested, "you're not going to church: I never thought you would
fib to anybody, least of all to Mungo." "I'm

not fibbing," she replied. "He knows nothing at all about church except that it is a place to which he can't go. I use the language he understands, and it is perfectly clear to him." Poor Mungo continued to bark at inappropriate times and to whirl whenever his mistress "returned from church," till blindness, and then feeblemindedness made life so evidently a burden to him, that a merciful ashman guided him painlessly to the land where good little dogs go at last.

Into this cottage came as a guest from time to time Miss Mary Webster Whipple, a cousin of Mr. Whipple, and a grand-niece of Daniel Webster. When I knew the cottage Miss Whipple was giving herself to a branch of the Indian lace-work, which had been started by Miss Sibyl Carter. Occasionally she would come out into the white man's country to gladden the lives of her friends and to lay in a supply of necessary clothes. She came with the latest news of

the Indians, vividly showing their pathos
and their dignity. She told once of a visit
which an old Indian paid her when she was
ill. "I hadn't been in church for some
time," she said; "so I asked him about the
sermon which he had heard last." "Was it
good?" she asked. "O yes," he answered
slowly, "very good. It was about the Trinity. I never knew what the Trinity meant;
now I know." Miss Whipple was instantly
alert. "Well," she said briskly, "I never
understood; tell me." "Well," he answered:
"it is this way: Trinity means three: there
is God—and Christ—and the devil—and
they are all pulling different ways." One
Winter I had been asked to write an article
on Indian children for a missionary magazine. Naturally I appealed to Miss Whipple for "copy." Quickly the reply came
giving me characteristic incidents. "But
really," she added, "you must ask Susie"—
referring to her colleague in the work—"she
sees more high lights than I do." But Miss

Whipple herself saw the romance and the charm in the old race. It is true she laughed over them, as when, for example, a certain Indian complained about the lace-making because his wife was obliged to wash her hands three times a day. On the other hand her eyes would fill with tears as she related some story of the devotion of "Good Thunder" and of other Indian saints. She too saw the high lights.

On one flight from the wilderness, she took charge of a small fourth cousin. Being an only child, he was somewhat spoiled, though altogether interesting, an exceedingly nice little boy, of whom she was very fond. Sometimes she meted out such discipline as she thought his absent parents would approve. Then she dipped into the psychology of her novel experience. "When I begin to spank him," she confessed, "I am sorry for him. Then, when he resists, I fall to work in earnest—and I enjoy it."

I think I never knew anyone who so

MARY WEBSTER WHIPPLE.

quickly read the thoughts of those who talked with her. Her eyes were always dancing with intelligence, and seemed to be looking into all the corners of one's mind. One day I chanced to speak of a very agreeable person who never seemed to get anywhere in particular. "Don't you think," I began—— "Yes I do," cried Miss Whipple. And that subject was finished. She knew all I was going to say!

That she might have the utmost to give, she spent the minimum upon her clothes. So the people who sewed for her were not among the clever. One morning she came back to the cottage the picture of misery: "O Cousin Mary," she wailed, "one sleeve was in backwards, and I must go again." Mrs. Whipple crisply intimated that one should not be bothered by such mundane trifles: the austerity was evident. "Yes, Cousin Mary," admitted Miss Whipple, "you're probably right. I suppose this is the sort of thing St. Paul would have called light afflictions!" Then suddenly the humility vanished. "But what," she exclaimed, "did St. Paul know about anything so exasperating! If he wanted a new suit, all he had to do was to go downtown and buy a sheet—it was sure to fit!"

Both these voices have long been silent; and I know not who sits in the vine-covered cottage to-day. But I do know that more delightful women never sat either in cottage or in palace; and someway, I am sure, their self-forgetting kindness goes on, to bless and help those who knew them here, and those for whom the joy of a new life is keener because they are part of it.

A BOY I KNEW

A BOY I KNEW

ONE November morning, more than twenty years ago, I learned that a boy had been born in the house of one of my friends. Wishing to express my own pleasure in the event, I went to a book shop and bought a little red Prayer Book, which I thought would be attractive to extreme youth, and took it as my first birthday gift to the baby. From that day I watched this boy.

He had hardly begun to develop before it was evident that one of his qualities was to be a sense of humour. His eyes were direct, black, and twinkling. A member of his household loved order extravagantly. One day, after the boy had left his toys strewn about the library, he returned from a walk to find them all put away. "Mother," he confided, "this room is as neat as a cemetery." At another time, just before Christmas, he came into this same library to find it cluttered with paper, string, and parcels destined to be gifts. "My aunt," he said, with a sweep of his hand, "doesn't like me to leave my things out. This is the difference between tweedledum and tweedledee."

Spending most of his time with his elders, he was apt to have the feeling that the little people he saw in the streets were several feet shorter than himself. I remember seeing him lean over the back of a low phaeton, where he was waiting while his mother was making a call, and, from this safe vantage-ground, his eyes snapping as usual, he made half-insulting, half-patronizing remarks to a group of children who were playing nearby. I mention this because I feared at the time that he might grow up to be a snob. My fears, as you will see, were groundless.

He was taken, as a matter of course, to

church and Sunday-school as early as possible. Coming home from Sunday-school
one morning, he was asked what he had
learned in the infant school. "Well," he
said, "I learned about a man named Stevens,
and I must say I didn't like him. He talked
too much. And the people didn't like him
either, so they threw stones at him; and then,
while they were throwing the stones, a man
named Saul came up and stole his clothes."
A psychologist might deduce a good deal
from this tale, both as to the teaching of the
Bible and as to the frank criticism of childhood.

He was a real boy, giving his parents the
usual anxieties. But besides being good by
the sanest sort of judgment, he was also religious. One afternoon, when the snow was
deep, he was told that he might play out
of doors provided he was careful not to get
wet and was at home promptly at five
o'clock, and that, after supper he might go
out for a little, with his dear friend the cook,

to coast. Five o'clock came. It was growing dark. But the boy did not come. At six, his mother, somewhat anxious, met him in the darkness at the door. He had been spending the afternoon in drifts, and was wet to the skin. The verdict came instantly that he must go at once to bed and have his supper there, and that there should be no coasting. Smitten with grief, he made his way to his room through the kitchen and up the back stairs. That was for the purpose of extracting comfort from the cook. His mother understood, and went the other way to meet him at the top of the stairs. When the lower door opened, the little figure, sobbing, kneeling on step by step, came slowly up, praying on each stair, "O Lord, give my mother a kind heart; give my mother a kind heart." It was the Scala Santa in modern form. His mother afterwards questioned whether perhaps she ought not to have strengthened his faith by changing her verdict; but a sound theology would

A BOY I KNEW.

approve her remaining steadfast in her loving discipline.

One morning he went into an upper chamber, and, after locking himself in, and, according to his custom, playing that he was Robinson Crusoe or some other enticing person, he felt the gnawings of hunger and wished to ask if it were not time for luncheon. Then to his dismay he could not turn the lock. By loud calling he made known his predicament, and all the women of the household put their minds upon the problem. They made suggestions at the door. They stood under the window and wondered how the room might be reached, and finally decided to wait until his father returned, that he might get a ladder and so mount to the desert island. During all this turmoil and discussion the boy stood in the window, sending out peals of laughter upon the Spring air. His mother and the others were perplexed because he was not frightened by his isolation. His father, returning, promptly took up the burden, borrowed a ladder, and was about to mount when the boy, amid paroxysms of laughter, said in his slow drawl, "Father, don't you think it would be better if I took the key out and threw it down to you, and you opened the door from the other side?"

He yearned to be a chorister, and, being rejected straightway by the choirmaster because he had neither ear nor voice, went off silently to a music teacher and confided in her the depth of his trouble, asking her please to develop his voice. She also knew without delay that he never could sing; but her heart was so touched by his plea that day after day she listened to his hopeless exercises, and then at last convinced him that he never could be a chorister.

Very early he decided upon his lifework. The horse, the garden, the gardener, were immediately his boyish delight. His heart was set upon being a farmer. He raised chickens. He sold The Saturday Evening

Post to increase his live-stock. And his methods were modern; he talked of incuba- tors. On a Saturday afternoon one of his aunts, coming home, detected a smell of smoke in the empty house. At last, opening the door from the kitchen to the cellar, she was overwhelmed with black clouds. The gardener, chancing to enter, swiftly ran down with pails of water, exclaiming each time as he returned for more, "Dat boy! Dat boy!" It proved that the boy had con- ceived the idea that a little straw on the top of the furnace would make an incubator, and there he had deposited a dozen eggs, expect- ing in due time to see the chickens fly down from their birthplace. When he came home that night, he learned how narrowly he had escaped destroying his home; but his sorrow was for another reason. "O mother," he cried, as he threw himself into her arms, "it was my beautiful surprise for your birthday, and now it is all spoiled!"

When the boy was ten years old, I moved

away from the town where he lived; and a
few days before my departure he and the
phaeton were lent to me to make certain
country calls; and a very diverting afternoon it was. We talked of all sorts of subjects. I asked him if he would not like to
be a minister. After probing with some care
my own satisfaction in my life-work, he said
that he thought that his father and mother
would probably like very much to have him
become a minister, but that he hardly saw
his way to it. He felt sure that he must
be a farmer. "I suppose," he said with a
sigh, "that I shall have to go to Harvard
College because my aunts insist on it; but
after that I am going to Amherst Agricul-
tural College." Just at this point, as we
were driving by a farm, he pointed to an
object, asking me in a tentative way if I
knew what it was. I ventured to say that
it was a harrow, at which he looked at me
with warm approval, asking, "How did you
know?" I answered by asking him how he

happened to know what it was. "Oh," he
replied, "of course *I* know; but I don't
understand how a minister should know what
a harrow is." As the afternoon progressed,
we became more and more nearly the same
age, and he took certain liberties which made
it clear to me that I seemed to him no older
than himself. It was delightful. Then suddenly his conscience smote him, and he let
the lines drop, a far-off look coming into his
eyes. "My!" he exclaimed, "I wonder if my
mother would think that I had been respect-
ful." Whereupon I laughed so long that
the relationship was immediately restored.

After this I did not see the boy for several years. I heard from him indirectly, and
my interest did not waver. In due time he
was sent to a school sufficiently near my new
home to allow him to come and spend part
of his Easter holiday with me. The little
boy had vanished, and, though he was only
thirteen, he had the stature of a man. He
talked freely of all his old enthusiasms. I

fear I teased him by talking blatantly of a rival school. He tried to be loyal under the circumstances, both to me and to his school, saying, with a pensive smile, "Well, I should like our headmaster to ask you to preach, but I am afraid some of these things you talk about wouldn't be acceptable to the fellows." Sitting with me in my study, he looked it over with mild approbation. "This is a nice room," he said, "but it is only about half as big as our headmaster's." He talked, one night at dinner, about his loyalty to the West, and was covered with confusion when he could not remember, upon being questioned, who the governor of his State was. It was afterwards explained by a member of his family that this was much to his credit, since this particular governor was not a person whom anyone should remember. I took him, on this Easter visit, into the church to hear the rehearsal of the Sunday evening music. As we sat down in a pew, a remarkable voice leapt to a high note with marvellous ease, and the boy, unmusical as he was, knew that something had happened. "That's pretty good," he whispered to me; "I think our headmaster would let him sing in the chapel, if you sent him up." Then, as the voice went still higher, with its clear notes, the boy again whispered, "Where does he come from?" I named a State not far from his own. He looked again, observing for the first time that the singer's hair was rather long. "Ah," he exclaimed, "from the West, is he? Well, one thing I must say, that hair doesn't do the West any credit."

Months passed. I heard from the boy's parents that the reports from his school varied. He was often much more interested in playing games and in prowling about the country, studying the wonderful world of out-of-doors, than he was in his books; but a beseeching letter from home clinched the headmaster's suasion, and the marks rapidly improved.

Then one day in the following fall I re-

ceived the message that the boy was danger-
ously ill. Before any who had known him
all his years could reach him, he was dead.
Out of apparently robust and vigorous
health, he had been taken, with scarcely a
warning, to another life. As I talked with
his schoolmasters on the morning of the
funeral, I learned that each was glad when
it came the boy's turn to sit near him at
table; for while the boys from the city talked
of the things of the city, this boy talked of
the open country, the birds, the things growing by the road, and the interesting people
one met by stone walls. Going into his room,
we found there the symbols of his character.
There were the photographs of the people
at home; carefully folded away was a bill-
head, bearing the boy's name, and describing
him as a dealer in poultry and farm produce
[(a bit of printing which he had done
privately the last summer, when he had sold
certain results of his garden and chicken-
coop) ; here also I saw upon the table the

little red Prayer Book which he had still kept and used; and then there were all the trifles that a boy keeps in his pocket and by his bedside. Yet as we looked upon the form, tall and sturdy, it was hard to believe that the spirit had vanished while he was still a boy. There came visions of what such a life must be in the larger freedom, prepared to live and therefore surely living. Some-one said, "He looks a brave young warrior;" another corrected, "A happy warrior;" and still another, "Unspotted from the world."

A younger brother, discovering his mother weeping over an article about the boy, brought his word of consolation. "This story," he began, "says that God has taken him to other fields." He paused. "Now," argued the little philosopher, "he is probably ploughing for God—and you know he would love that."

A MINNESOTA DOCTOR

A MINNESOTA DOCTOR

DURING the first Fall which I spent in Minnesota I went to a convocation in Red Wing. Red Wing is a town among the hills on the Mississippi River, a picturesque situation with beautiful outlook. In the early days of the town three graduates of Hobart College decided to throw in their lot with its history—a clergyman named Edward Randolph Welles, and two physicians, Augustine Boyer Hawley and Charles Nathaniel Hewitt. The two physicians were, with a lawyer, Eli T. Wilder, the chief pillars of the parish of which Mr. Welles was the rector. Four strong and able men, they were typical of the young professional men who were coming in those days from the Northeastern

States of our country to make the substantial citizenship of the great Northwest. They stood for old American traditions, education, refinement, and character. They made Red Wing an enviable neighbourhood, and they made of Christ Church one of the notable churches in a whole group of dioceses. With the vision which might have been expected of such men, a triangular plot of ground in the very centre of the town was secured, and a stone church, on good Gothic lines, was built. No one who entered Red Wing could fail to see Christ Church, and, seeing it, stop to marvel at its commanding situation and its reverent appeal.

With the limitations of Massachusetts still upon me I was frankly surprised to find in a community only a score or so of years older than myself a sense of history and a people's pride in its past. Mr. Wilder had become a judge, was recognized as the chief layman of the diocese, and for many sessions had been a leader in the General Convention.

Dr. Hawley, who had studied medicine in Edinburgh and Paris, and who had given an affectionate ministry to the sick and suffering of Red Wing, had been dead eighteen years. Mr. Welles had become Bishop of Wisconsin; he, too, had been long dead. The remaining member of the distinguished group was Dr. Hewitt, of whom I wish especially to speak in this chapter.

Dr. Hewitt was my host on this my first visit to Red Wing. I knew by hearsay that he was full of interest and charm, but I was not prepared for the real man. In the late afternoon I went up to his gate. I found myself before a low wooden house among the trees. Instantly even the house bristled with individuality: it had what we strangely call atmosphere. With all its modesty and simplicity one knew that somebody who was somebody lived within it. It is more than twenty years ago that I made that visit. But I have still the vivid impression of the dining-room where a group of people, the

nicest of the nice, sat down for dinner—a
little early because the first service of the
convocation was to be that night. There was
the sparkle of friendliness and humour passing over the table, with now and again a
brilliant, half-caustic flash from the host,
which made me at least wish that convoca-
tions would never have opening sessions the
first night, and that we might sit indefinitely
at that feast of fast-flying talk, where eating
was of little moment.

After the opening session of the convocation the men went into the library for more
talk, which lasted far into the night. This
room was the typical room in a house full
of personality. Books were everywhere, and
among the books at one end of the room
were the pipes of an organ. The host told
the story of the organ. He loved the music
of the Church, and around this organ he
had, on Sunday afternoons, gathered the
boys of the town who could sing. He had
taught them hymns and canticles—and good

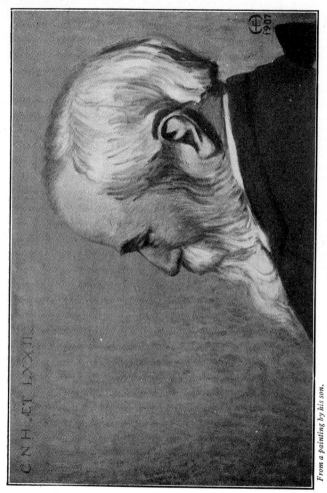

C·N·H· ÆT· LXXII·

From a painting by his son.

CHARLES NATHANIEL HEWITT.

manners. He had scolded them, laughed at them, loved them. Christ Church, Red Wing, was a conservative parish, and it did not believe that boys should lead the music in the church; but the day came at last when the boys in Dr. Hewitt's library were told that they might put on surplices, march into Christ Church, and sit in the choir. And then the whole parish knew what Dr. Hewitt had been doing through the Sunday afternoons of many years. I doubt if any choristers ever had such thorough preparation as these boys of Red Wing before their first appearance in a chancel. I have often thought that I should like to have seen Dr. Hewitt's face that first Sunday morning when his own boys sang the music of the service in the church which he and his friends had built.

After all the years I can remember some of the things Dr. Hewitt said that November night. One of the guests in the house was an enthusiastic mountain climber, and described the perils from which, during the past Summer, he and some friends had narrowly escaped. I remember asking about a college friend who had lost his life in the mountains two years before. The same guest knew every detail of his exploit. It was a thrilling description, and we sat spellbound—all but Dr. Hewitt. He sat stiffly in his chair, a look half of pity, half of displeasure on his face. "Do you call that heroism?" he asked. "I call it waste of life. A man has no right to run such risks except for a worthy object—an object which helps someone, or pushes on some great cause." Arguments were brought up to plead for the spirit of adventure, the advance of scientific discovery, the inculcation of courage in a soft age—but he would have none of them. Life to him seemed so full of necessary perils that the strong man must save himself scrupulously for the inevitable crisis. He bit savagely into the subject; and the enthusiast for the mountains allowed the conversation to come down to the inhabited valleys.

Soon we were talking about sermons, and this was by Dr. Hewitt's own choice. He began to talk about preachers who ventilated their intellectual processes. "I trust my clergyman," he said; "I want him to settle all his doubts and difficulties at home. When he stands up to preach his sermon I want him to give me the conclusions he has reached. I want to know what he believes." We smiled; for we suspected that if the trusted rector happened to hit upon conclusions which were not fairly in harmony with the conclusions which the vigorous and thoughtful doctor had reached in his library there would be a brisk asking of questions in front of the post-office the next morning, and peppery argument interspersed with amusing flings, now at things too old, and again at things too new.

Dr. Hewitt had been at one time the chief executive officer of the State board of health.

In a certain epidemic of smallpox he made it his task to see that every man, woman, and child in Minnesota was vaccinated. He told us that night of his experience in visiting a monastery, the brethren of which had thus far refused to submit to the order of the board of health. Dr. Hewitt himself went to the monastery to see that every monk was vaccinated. He reached the remote building one bleak Winter evening after a long railway journey. He was admitted to a hall which was just a little colder than the world out of doors. He was told that in due time the abbot would see him. Cold and hungry, the doctor waited for more than an hour, expecting every moment that the tomb-like hall would open and he should be admitted again to life. When at length the door opened and a brother announced that the abbot would now see him, Dr. Hewitt's temper was running high. He did not know exactly what he would say, but he was sure that such an abbot as this, who certainly knew of his waiting guest, should receive some punishment. The abbot received the physician with a dignity several degrees more frigid than the hall. He evidently wished to impress him with the folly and temerity of any interference of the State with Holy Church. This dignity of the abbot was quickly punctured by Dr. Hewitt, who took up the parable: "I want to tell you," he said, "that I am familiar with the rules of your order. The first rule is hospitality. You have grossly disobeyed it. You have kept me waiting in a cold hall for more than an hour." One could instinctively feel the collapse of the abbot as the story was told. Immediately the abbot apologized and begged forgiveness: there was no more effort to play Canossa. "Everything will be done to make you comfortable," said the abbot sweetly, "and to-morrow you will meet the brethren in the chapter and we shall confer about the object of your visit."

The next morning the doctor found him-

self in a large room with the monks seated
about the walls, the abbot in his seat of
authority. When all was ready the abbot
announced, "One of the brethren will now
read a paper which will convince you, Dr.
Hewitt, that vaccination is not only useless,
but wrong." First amazed, then indignant,
the doctor gradually fell back upon the
humour of the situation. Suddenly a
thought came to him, and he smiled with
great joy; for he saw that the monastery was
delivered into his hand. The last part of
the paper he did not hear. He was thinking of more cheerful things than smallpox.
When the reader sat down there was a hum
of approval, and all seemed satisfied that
nothing could be said in reply. Dr. Hewitt
waited a moment, and then rose calmly.
"This has been very interesting," he said;
"I, a physician, have listened to a paper
about medicine written by a theologian.
Now I propose to do for you what you have
kindly done for me. I ask you, as

theologians, to listen to me while I, a physician, speak to you on a grave matter of theology. There is one of your doctrines which I as physician know to be wholly impossible and I can prove it to you. I am sure that I can make clear to you its utter. . . . " With that there was a shout from every corner of the room, "O doctor, vaccinate us!" From abbot to youngest brother, there was a throwing up of sleeves, and arms were made ready for the officer of the State. The doctor, saying no more of theology, fell to work.

In course of time the migration from Northeastern America ceased, and a new migration began — from Northwestern Europe, especially Scandinavia. When members of the Church of Sweden entered Red Wing they found a dignified church with a well-ordered service, which seemed more like home than anything else in the new world. Thus new parishioners mingled among the old, and the foundations laid by four good men with generations of Americans behind them served for the happy superstructure in which Americans of a newer citizenship have shared.

Dr. Hewitt was the last of these founders to finish his work in this life. Eight years ago he joined his three friends; perhaps they together have sought out some celestial frontier which they can, by their presence and their deeds, make happier for men, who, through them, shall become joyfully eager to give worship to God.

SAMUEL HART

SAMUEL HART

ONE of the most impressive recurring moments in the General Convention for many sessions has been the time, day by day, when it has been announced in the House of Clerical and Lay Deputies that a message from the House of Bishops was about to be received. Everyone has stood, and Dr. Samuel Hart, the Secretary of the House of Bishops, has walked slowly from the western door to the President's desk at the eastern end of the church or hall. He has always carried the document at exactly the same angle, and has never varied his step. For a man abounding in humour and also exceedingly modest, it was only respect for his task which could have kept him invariably serious and dignified, and at the same time unconscious of himself and wholly unembarrassed, as he performed a trying duty. This solemn procession of one has told those who have cared to think about it characteristic news of Samuel Hart.

Long before I ever met Dr. Hart I heard of him from students of Trinity College, Hartford. He taught Latin there, and won the respect and affection of all the men. They called him, behind his back, "Sammie Hart"—which meant that they liked him very much indeed. One of them told me that when at Chapel they read in the Psalter, "He maketh my feet like harts' feet," they always turned and looked at Professor Hart. They recognized in him an accurate scholar, whose influence upon them was potent for good. They heard of his regular visits to the hospital. He did his countless kindnesses with the utmost quietness: they admired his simplicity. When he went back to a college commencement recently he met an old pupil whom he had not seen for many

years. "Well," he said, "how are things going with you, Jimmie?" The man straightened, and answered: "Oh, very well indeed,
Dr. Hart; I never expected my business
could have prospered as it has. Everything
seems to have come my way." "I'm very
glad," said the kind old friend; "but I didn't
mean quite that." Then suddenly he broke
off, and Dr. Hart's eyes turned earnestly
upon him, as he said, "Jimmie, do you say
your prayers?" I rather think that the man
did say his prayers; but if he had grown careless, the thought that someone cared enough
to break through the natural reserves of life
—that someone being a person whose right
to ask pointed questions he recognized—the
old habit would have begun again, never
again to stop.

Later Dr. Hart went to Berkeley Divinity School, to be first Professor of Theology,
and then Dean. He had always been close
to Bishop Williams, and it meant much to
the loyal follower of the great Bishop to be

carrying on the School which the Bishop
had founded, and to be living even in the
Bishop's old house. There is a tale that when
the Bishop wished this favourite son in the
Faith to be elected to any office in the gift
of the Diocesan Convention, such as a place
on the Standing Committee or on the delega-
tion to the General Convention, he would
stand in the door of the meeting place, and
say as he greeted each clergyman, "How do
you do, my dear brother;" and then add in
a whisper, as if it were a great secret, "Vote
for Sam Hart." And "Sam Hart" was always elected! Everyone felt that when Dr.
Hart succeeded to an office which was perhaps the largest part of Bishop Williams's
life-work, the Bishop must have been whis-
pering the directions through the celestial
spaces.

When I came to live in a neighbouring
diocese, Dean Hart laid hold upon me, and
brought me down to Middletown to give
occasional lectures to the students. I always

stayed with him in the big old house, when I made my visits to the School; and I came to look forward to these visits as bright spots in my working year. The house itself was interesting. Washington had slept in it, and its architecture was worthy of such an honour. But, more than that, was the thought of Bishop Williams, whom it seemed exactly to fit. Dr. Hart lived alone, and we ate together in the old dining-room. I was always glad when there was no other guest, for we were apt to sit talking, at the table, long after we had finished the simple and excellent repast. He was the sort of man with whom one instantly felt at home. With wide-spreading knowledge and generous sympathy, he talked of the things in which one was most absorbed. If he touched on his own hobbies, he did it with an amused chuckle, to show that he knew what a queer old fellow he was. I asked him what he was reading that was particularly inspiring. "Oh," he said, "a whole raft of books on

Halley's Comet, and Dr. Swete's new book on *The Holy Spirit in the Ancient Church.*" Then he talked about both in a way which showed that though he was a thorough theologian, the fresh air of other interests blew in and out among his ancient doctrines, and made them alive and wholesome.

He was a fine type of Anglican theologian, steeped in the traditions of the English Church, devoted to its order and beauty. In his stall in the Chapel he kept a Hebrew Bible and a Greek Testament, that he might follow the Lessons in the original. He liked Morning and Evening Prayer just as they were, and resented the addition of many hymns. He pleaded for a dignified phraseology in speaking of the functions of the Church. He felt that to speak of the Holy Communion as "the celebration" was irreverent; and he shuddered when he heard young clergymen talking of being "priested." He thought people might take time to say "celebration of the Holy

Samuel Hart.

Communion," and "ordained to the priest-
hood." I asked the privilege of being present at one of his lectures on Liturgics at
the School. One could not help being impressed by the reverent way he turned the
leaves of the Prayer Book as he talked.
There was not only the minute technical information which he gave his men about
authorship and date and doctrine: there was
also the historical allusion; and, still more,
the revelation of his own devout reaction. It
was eminently appropriate that he was the
official "Custodian of the Book of Common
Prayer." He loved every comma in the
book.

He never paraded his friendships as he
talked; but he had deep intimacies. He and
Bishop Doane of Albany exchanged constant letters in Latin. One found this out
only by accident, as he spoke of devising
some Latin word to designate a modern in-
vention. He had profound regard for Dr.
William Huntington, and always spoke of

him with peculiar earnestness. But the personality beyond and above all other friends was his master, Bishop Williams. That was a fellowship of which I seldom heard him talk; but I knew that he never forgot him, in all his thinking and teaching.

He was Connecticut condensed into one man. Except to go to the General Convention, he seemed never to go out of the State. He was elected Bishop of Vermont, but he promptly declined to go away. His chief journeying was, first, between Hartford and Saybrook; and, then, between Middletown and Saybrook; for it was in Saybrook that his mother lived. He had all the Connecticut humour and ingenuity and sense of order. Had he not been the soul of honesty he could have even made wooden nutmegs. He exulted in Connecticut history, and Connecticut traditions, and Connecticut idioms. He knew many of the little parishes tucked away in the hills which everyone else seemed to have forgotten. He told me once that an eminent layman of New Haven had a Sunday or two before happened to spend the day in a decaying little village where our Church services continued to be held. The layman put his usual Sunday morning offering on the plate, and thought no more of it. But the next morning he was informed that the vestry of the little church had come to see him. "We have come to thank you," they said, "for your help to our parish: it is the largest offering we have ever received." It was two dollars. Dr. Hart laughed his inimitable laugh as he described the vestryman who passed the plate to the stranger, and nervously watched to see what he would drop upon it; but there was something like a sob in his voice when he finished the story. It was all an instance of the humour and the pathos of his dear Connecticut.

Dr. Hart's life was, for the most part, lived in the quiet of a scholar's retirement. But from his watch-tower he looked out upon the larger world. He disposed of showy superficiality, when he saw it apparently succeeding in this man or that, by a coy allusion, never bitter, never self-complacent, only amused. He asked how the people who had the power of choice could have chosen to lead their cause a man who was palpably not at all fitted: didn't they know, or didn't they care? It was quite alarming to discover how much a man living in a somewhat detached community could know of everything and everybody. The judgments which went out upon people who felt secure upon the pedestals of their importance seemed in some way to have an authority which the louder verdict of men and groups in the public eye could not have.

The humour of Dr. Hart was full of originality and spontaneity. His last conspicuous duty was to the General Convention of 1916 in St. Louis. The sessions were to be held in a garish hall called Moolah Temple. When he went out with others to arrange details for the Convention with the local committee, he stood at the door of Moolah Temple and looked in. Instantly came the short chuckle from Dr. Hart, as he said, "Give thy servant two mules' burden of earth, when my master goeth into the house of Rimmon!"

The old house in Middletown has one more association with the past. Some of us will value it most of all because one whose memory we shall ever cherish lived and died in it, with the simplicity of a scholar and a saint.

HENRY VAUGHAN

HENRY VAUGHAN

IN years to come one of the men to whom America will be grateful is Henry Vaughan. He was the architect of the chapels of two of our great American schools, St. Paul's and Groton. Three of the Chapels of the Tongues, clustered about the apse of the New York Cathedral, are the result of his reverent genius. Most of all, the Cathedral in Washington will be wholly his; since, by wise foresight, he was induced to make working drawings of the entire structure, though it was evident that perhaps not for generations could the huge church be finished.

Few people ever saw Henry Vaughan. I cannot remember hearing that he ever made a speech or appeared on any public platform. The memory which most people, even of his own generation, can have of him, therefore, is what they have seen of him in his churches. These churches speak clearly of the character of the architect who thought them out. They all have rare beauty, but the continuing impression which they give is peace. There is exquisite detail, but there is also much plain surface. There is nothing grotesque. The spirit of mediæval art is there, but is perfectly assimilated in a devout builder of the nineteenth and twentieth centuries. I cannot remember any grinning creatures crouching even in obscure corners. There was nothing forced or affected in his ornamentation. A restraint which was something more than good taste marked his work.

I was once rector of a New England parish which had chosen him for its architect. The original building was on fairly good lines, but quite different from anything he would have done. He wrote frequent letters, always with his own hand, and the problem was often talked over face to face. I think he never complained of the obvious faults of the building. We were eager to have three wheel windows changed to rose windows by such noble tracery as we knew that he could design; he gave us sketches, but he warned us that the beauty of rose windows was not at all in the tracery but in the quality of the glass. We had money for a modest tower, and he set to work to draw for us what could be done for thirty thousand dollars. When it was discovered that the lowest estimate was more than fifty thousand, he blamed himself for stupidity, and straightway set to work again. But, once having seen the drawing which he had first made, the Vestry could not be satisfied with anything less; and the Parish waits for it. Perhaps it will come, after the War, as a thank offering for Peace—and for Henry Vaughan!

When one came to know him, one found

the source of the spirit which dominated his churches. He consented to design for us a pulpit in memory of a former rector, and I wished to talk it over with him. I found him at length on one of the upper floors of a Boston office building. It was an insignificant office, small and bare. He was standing at work behind a tall desk. He looked like one of the Pre-Raphaelites—somewhat as I imagine Burne-Jones looked, only a little more remote from the world. His face, with its solemn eyes, regular features, and full beard, was instantly arresting. The gentleness of his bearing and voice was typical of his consideration. He waited patiently to hear what must often have seemed to him the crudity of the wishes of the eager patron. He honestly tried to see what one had in mind and to work it out. Thus doubtless he instilled humility into the amateur, and his suggestions, tentatively made, were immediately seen to be what one was subconsciously striving to attain. Thus

HENRY VAUGHAN.

I have felt that his building has often expressed not only the spirit of Henry Vaughan, but also, by his sympathy, the spirit of the earnest giver. In many ways the most beautiful church of his workmanship is the Chapel of St. Boniface, one of the chapels of the New York Cathedral. I know how much the givers, Mr. and Mrs. Bowdoin, of blessed memory, put of themselves into the happy project; and I seem to find that its simplicity, graciousness, and sincerity are, through Mr. Vaughan's skill, the revelation of what he saw in them. He had no artistic conceit to immortalize his own ideas: with such dreams as God gave him, he fused the dreams of those who pleaded for his help, and the unity which resulted was evidence of a generous willingness to listen as well as to teach.

The little bare office in Boston was typical of his unworldliness. It seemed a shrine, in which no earthly or sordid thoughts could dwell. And the man who stood behind the tall desk was like a saint out of a picture. I cannot recall any word concerning fees. Of course his bills came in due time, and were duly paid. But I cannot think of him in connection with money. It was altogether plain that his art was not a business, but a vocation, with all the sacredness which attaches to a work imposed by God's command. I don't know whether he was rich or poor. I think he didn't care.

I am told that, though he could have had almost unlimited commissions, he never undertook work which he could not personally supervise. This was the reason for his small office and his small staff of assistants. Everything which seemed to come from him did come from him. This virtue had its defects. Through his delay in furnishing working drawings for a church, the cost of materials so increased that the one hundred and fifty thousand dollars collected and adequate at the time the commission was given him, was, when his designs were ready, less than enough by fifty thousand. If money was nothing to him, those for whom he planned were also obliged to learn to subordinate it. He was unquestionably slow. But only so could he work. And so, inevitably, many turned away in discouragement to seek help elsewhere.

I learned to know him best through his building the pulpit (of which I have already spoken) in memory of a beloved rector who had served his parish for twenty-eight years. The task was relatively slight, but Mr. Vaughan gave not only to the plans, but to the construction, as much interest as if he were building a whole cathedral. He was careful to regard the spirit of the man who was to be commemorated. Around the pulpit were to be the figures of St. Paul, St. Chrysostom, Savonarola, Latimer, and Brooks, representing preaching in the Apostolic Church, the Greek, Latin, English, and American Churches. He urged me to come to see these figures in clay be-

fore the carving began, so that they would
surely be just as we should like to have
them. We met one day at the factory, and
the Oberammergau carver took us into the
room where he was working. Mr. Vaughan
and I stood before the five clay figures. St.
Paul we knew by his sword and his book;
Chrysostom was sufficiently evident; Savonarola held up his cross, and the familiar
outlines of his face proclaimed him; Latimer stood with his lantern. The fifth
figure was enveloped in a cope; a high mitre
was on his head; a pastoral staff was in one
hand; and the other hand, encased in a glove
with a cross upon its back, was giving a
blessing. Mr. Vaughan and I were both
puzzled. Suddenly it dawned upon us that
the face in the midst of all this adornment
was the face of Phillips Brooks! I laughed;
but Mr. Vaughan was very serious, as he
turned to the carver with the gentle explanation, " I hardly think this will do: you
know he never wore any of these things."

It was at length arranged to send to the carver a photograph of an American bishop wearing the rochet and chimere of the ordinary Anglican costume. Meantime the carver turned to me, with a smile. "You know," he said, "I admired him so mooch, I vanted him to have everyting dere vas." "But you know," Mr. Vaughan expostulated, "he never wore them." "Vell, certainly," replied the old carver, with a shrug, "I tink he vears 'em now."

When the pulpit was done, Mr. Vaughan came to see it in the church; and he was satisfied. Through all the years, though it is a very small part of the work he did in the world, it will speak of the deeply religious nature, the gentleness, the genuineness, the humility of Henry Vaughan.

A PENNSYLVANIA HOME

A PENNSYLVANIA HOME

ONE of the unforgettable experiences of life is to enter a great home—that is, a home which is really a home, and is quite different from every other home. Long after the home is broken up, after the hallowed doorstep is touched only by strange and careless feet, after all the pictures and the books and the furniture have been divided amongst two or three generations of heirs, still the memory of that home stays in its unique nook in the mind. And so one surmises that never in all the life of man will there be a home like that again.

I have known at least one such home. I am told that I was carried to it as an infant; I remember it in recurring visits through my childhood; I saw it again and again through manhood. The last summer that it was a home I spent a fortnight in it; and I heard with a pang of its ultimate dismantling. I knew that there was a part of myself on which I must shut to the door, and turn the key in the lock. Henceforth there was only a memory. This was the home of Felix and Mary Brunot in Western Pennsylvania: it was a corner house of brick in Allegheny in the Winter; it was a wooden house amid wide acres in Verona in the Summer; but it was one home; for one beautiful personality was woven into the life of both, the united life of a marriage made in heaven.

As I grew to take them less for granted, I began to discover what elements made up the characters of these two people. Felix Brunot was the grandson of the beloved foster-brother of Lafayette. The two brothers together came to fight in the American Revolution, and Brunot re-

mained in America. Mary Brunot was the
daughter of an Englishman who had come
from Newcastle in the eighteenth century.
The chivalry of France and the reliability
of England strengthened each the other in
this American home. Then I learned of the
school days of Felix Brunot, spent under
the quick temper and varied genius of John
Henry Hopkins, rector and schoolmaster,
who later was Bishop of Vermont. Mrs.
Brunot went to a school in Philadelphia:
she often told me of the journeys over the
mountains before the days of railways, in
the cumbersome stage-coaches, the driver
lashing his horses, and the stage rushing
down the steep hills behind them, to what
seemed to the child certain destruction. The
outstanding recollection of these school-days
in Philadelphia, however, was the religious
awakening that came Sunday by Sunday as
she sat under the fiery eloquence of Dr.
Tyng. Hopkins and Tyng were, in their
individual way, quite as potent in the form-

ing of destiny as the racial strains of France and England: one might have been a Renaissance pope, encouraging and loving all the arts (only he loved and practised religion too), the other might have been a John the Baptist or a Savonarola.

The town house was filled with beautiful old things: mahogany, engravings, portraits, first editions—but there was no consciousness that they were there. They had, I suppose, been "handed down" from earlier times. Nothing new seemed to be bought, and there were no concessions to passing styles. The country house was furnished, evidently, in the simplest possible way in the taste of the year it was built—and so it remained to the end.

Felix Brunot, trained as a civil engineer, early dropping all professional and business interests to devote himself to philanthropy, seeing his inherited wealth increase in spite of his lavish giving, was a poet in face and word. Tall and straight, with a singularly

Photograph by F. Gutekunst.

FELIX REVILLE BRUNOT.

noble face crowned with long white hair, he looked a little like the pictures of Franz Lizst, only with a greater beauty and dignity. His low voice, his serene kindness, his sense of strength, his deep religious fervour, his unconscious grace, contributed to a personality quite different from any other that I have ever known. One discovered that he wrote verse: Mrs. Brunot would show anyone for whom she cared much, verses which he had written to her. If for instance she had placed an Easter card on his plate on Easter morning, the card would come back to her with his touching and loving words on the blank side, that the card might belong to both of them. With a good deal of the naturalist in him he saw what most men pass by.

Mary Brunot was also tall, with a corresponding dignity of presence. She looked as if she had been created to be the wife of Felix Brunot. As I first remember her she wore her soft and abundant hair with

little ringlets on either side of her face, but
these disappeared. A whimsical smile was
constantly playing about her mouth, and
her voice was rich and vibrant—a very unusual voice. Young people were just a little in awe of her: she seemed to them too
religious and strict. But all the influence
of Dr. Tyng could not rob her of her in-
nate humanism. She was patient when a
niece or a nephew giggled at family
prayers; and no ridiculous aspect of the
people about her escaped her. When she
laughed, she carried everything before her.
To please Mr. Brunot she would wear clothing of the finest stuffs: to please herself and
the Puritan within her, she had this clothing made with the most uncompromising
plainness. There is no doubt that she was
a quaint, as well as a stately, figure. A
young clergyman, on hearing Mrs. Brunot's
name spoken, said one day to Deaconess
Sibyl Carter (who loved Mrs. Brunot as
a daughter loves a mother), "Doesn't she

look as if she came out of the ark?" "Young man," said Miss Carter, the smile instantly fading from her face, "she is one of the two or three people in the world worthy of going *into* the ark!"

There were no sons and daughters in this home; but it was a rare day when there were not nieces and nephews. It was for most of them a good deal more than a second home. They said "Uncle" and "Auntie" without further designation. There was a sense of ownership on both sides close to parenthood. This was no silent home where the tears and laughter of children were absent: it was a Mecca for children. The coachman's children, too, came up from the lodge, in both town and country, every morning before breakfast, and shared in family prayers. Each guest, servant, and child took turns with the master and mistress, in reading a verse of the chapter; then after Mr. Brunot had read the prayers, the coachman's children stood in a row before Mrs. Brunot, and she heard them each say a verse from the Bible and a verse from a hymn. If they stumbled, she made light of it, and helped them through. Afterward she gave them a bit of gay advice and sent them off with the letters. It was hard for a guest to keep back the tears as he saw this relic of patriarchal simplicity, and thought what it must mean for the children all their lives long.

On Sunday afternoons these same children came into the drawing room to say verses and to hear chapters from a story book—first a boys' book, then a girls'. All the guests came in, and each said his verse with the children. Mrs. Brunot, who was always the reader, confessed how interested she became in the books; and the Dr. Tyng part of her wondered if it were quite right to read such interesting books on Sunday afternoon, but the humanism conquered. Then someone sat down at the little organ, and we sang one of Mr. Brunot's hymns;

and the nice children shook hands and went away.

The guests included chiefly bishops and other missionaries who were working hard in distant places. If they were not there to tell in person their varied experiences, there was apt to be, after breakfast, the reading of letters from the ends of the earth. It was not difficult to guess why there was rigid simplicity in this home: it was pleasanter to cheer up a hero in Africa or China than to have a new carpet. I remember that Mrs. Brunot once told me that one of her disciplines was to think what she would do if she woke up some morning stripped of every penny. She rather thought that she could start out blithely before noon to do someone's washing and to scrub down somebody's stairs—if only the neuralgia, to which she was subject, were not very bad. Indeed she thought she could be perfectly happy. Probably, for the moment, she forgot what would happen in Africa and China, if some worldly and selfish person acquired the money. For after Mr. Brunot's illness began, her business adviser was obliged to tell her from time to time that she had given away more than her income, and she must not be so dishonest as to overdraw her bank account.

One fall when Mr. Brunot was at his fishing club on Lake Erie, his boat upset, and he was for many hours in the cold water. Paralysis began, which, creeping farther and farther, robbed him of speech, and for thirteen years he was an invalid, pitiful, yet still serene. In his face was the same purity and grace, the same dignity and authority, but also a look of wonder and perplexity. His face, as he sat among us in his silence, was as the memory of a glorious day: we knew that he was only waiting for the end. Then Mrs. Brunot rose to the greatness of her love. She went to her own boards and meetings, she wrote all the letters which her interests and enthusiasms bade her write;

and then she did his work too. She spoke
for him, she wrote for him—though only the
deep love in his eyes could tell her what to
say: he could not write, he could not speak.
The separation called death came; but she
went on saying "we," when she spoke of all
her plans and work. "I suppose," she said,
"I ought to stop saying 'we'—but I cannot
help it." Of course her instinct to say it
was right.

The last visit I made was at Verona. Mrs.
Brunot, now quite alone, told me with a natural poise of all the beautiful past together
—of the courtship, of the experience on the
frontier, of Mr. Brunot's part in the civil
war when he all but gave his life in the
Sanitary Commission, of their summer
journeys over the Western plains to visit
wild Indian tribes, when Mr. Brunot was
President of the Indian Commission, of
days abroad and at home, of their friends
and heroes. I walked over the broad estate
at Verona, and remembered how Mr.

Brunot had led me by the hand when I was a child, showing me the rock-fountain he had builded with his own hands, the vista he had opened to the Allegheny, the cool spring under the hill. I remembered how, when I was nearly ready for my work, we went together the same familiar round; and he spoke affectionate words about my father, who had been his rector and friend, and added that if he had his life to live over, he would be in the Ministry too. I even went, by Mrs. Brunot's wish, to look again at the town house, and to pick out some of Mr. Brunot's books which I might like to keep for his sake. It was all just as I had remembered it from the beginning. Only it was becoming very far down town, and I knew that it must soon cease to be any-body's home. I went out again with Mrs. Brunot in her carriage, and she would stop in passing through some rough neighbour-hood to call dirty children up to the carriage window. She would laugh, say a few words to them, and then draw out of the pocket in the door a children's tract, which she was sure that they would like. I don't care much for tracts; but she knew children, and I am sure that she picked out tracts which were really interesting, and sane, and hopeful. I am sure that the children went home to tell their mother of the pretty old lady with the smile who had stopped to talk and to give them a little book—and the mother doubtless knew who it was, and read the story aloud, and thought of the day when she was sick and Mrs. Brunot had sent her good things to eat, and had eased the burden of living by quiet and cheering words. Tracts from such a source meant something.

And that last Summer there were the visitors. There were the brilliant and the wise, who sat in the drawing room and ate with Mrs. Brunot; and there were the very humble who wandered about the paths picking flowers and eating with the servants. These latter guests came from Mrs.

Brunot's various charitable institutions: she
wanted them to spend their day in the country in the way they would feel freest and
most comfortable. She herself would have
been glad to have them at her own table,
but her imagination told her how their ap-
petite would have been cramped. There
was a radiant democracy binding her to all
her fellows, but her sound sense never led
her to treating everybody alike. She was
inspired to do the thing each liked best. She
never went to town in the summer without
a huge bouquet in her hand. She would
give it away, bit by bit, in the hot and dirty
city, especially to girls sitting in the dreary
railway station, looking forlorn and home-
sick. Once more her imagination told her
what a woman's kindness might mean before the morning's sun shone again. She
was both a personality and an institution.
She had presided at so many boards that
she was a board of directors in herself.

The prosperous world about Mrs.

MARY H. BRUNOT.

Brunot, of which in ordinary circumstances she would have been a part, and from which she made no effort to separate herself, looked on with amusement and admiration. She simply had no time for anyone who was not doing something to help someone else. She didn't despise selfish people; she simply forgot that there were any such people. Yet, in a measure, she knew what went on in the world, and she said her emphatic word against any custom or usage which she felt to be wrong, however the world tolerated or encouraged it. One day she was telling an interesting and able woman, who lived near her, how wicked she thought it to play cards for prizes: it was, she thought, indistinguishably close to playing for money, which was exactly gambling, and nothing else. This lady found Mrs. Brunot's words so convincing that she regretted having accepted an invitation (which she felt that she must accept) to a house where she knew that cards were to be played. She said to herself that of course she could not win a prize, since she did not know even how to play the game. So far she was safe. Her husband assured her that the game was perfectly simple, the only rule to remember was, "Risk everything." She went, sat down, "risked everything," and came home with a large silver object—the first prize! She told me that she kept thinking of dear Mrs. Brunot's face, and while she laughed alone in her carriage, coming home, till the tears ran down her cheeks, she felt exactly as if she had broken into Mrs. Brunot's house and stolen all her silver.

Mrs. Brunot found the new ways which were coming over the Church very trying. A sermon on Jonah, frankly cognizant of higher criticism, quite upset her. After I was ordained, she would take me into a corner now and then and ask me the meaning of this or that which she had noticed in a service recently. "Why," she would say, "did the minister turn his back upon the congregation after his sermon? If it doesn't mean anything and 'he just does it,' it seems to me very bad manners. And if it does mean anything—I don't like it." At another time she told me of a missionary meeting for women in some city church. "There was a visiting bishop," she said, "who did very strange things which I never saw done before; and, dear me!" she added, "I hope our bishop didn't see him—for if he did, he'll be doing them too!"

She had her days of physical pain, and every day she was lonely without her dear companion of a lifetime; but she ran up and down the stairs like a girl, she went to her meetings, she drove through the familiar streets in town, and over the country roads. And then came the great change, fittingly enough, on an All Saints' Day. It seemed impossible for a moment to think of the world without her and the home which had been her background. And then the comfort came in the remembrance that some things on earth are so good and honourable that they are the promise of eternal realities. The maker of a home must be able to take the spirit of a home wherever she may go; and so we may venture to translate a certain august pledge of the Master into the assurance that the place to which He has led the way, is a place of many homes. If so, one such home of perpetual joy, I am sure I know.

BISHOP HARE

BISHOP HARE

ONE Autumn evening in the later Eighties there was a public meeting in Sanders Theatre in Cambridge in behalf of the American Indian. As an American youth I was glad of a chance to hear about the Indian; but the chief attraction of the meeting for me was that Bishop Hare, whom I had long wished to see, was to speak. He had then been Bishop of South Dakota for many years. We expected that we should see a man touched with the rough force of the frontier, who, in spite of his gentle upbringing in Philadelphia, would be what we thought a man must become after fifteen or twenty years as Bishop to the Indians. But he looked and spoke only as the exquisite gentleman he was. He might have belonged to the tribe of cultivated Americans who refuse to travel west of Buffalo. One who did not know, would never have dreamed that he made it his chief business to travel back and forth over the plains ministering to the simple needs of the aboriginal American.

I can still recall the surprise expressed by certain distinguished members of the Harvard faculty that a man could give his first attention to Indians and yet speak to a Harvard audience as hardly anyone had spoken for years. There was an elegance and distinction, together with perfect simplicity, about his appearance, bearing, and utterance, which one associated only with perpetual contact with great centres. The dazed professors were rather nettled that they hadn't known about this unique person before.

I can see him, in my memory, as he stood that night before a somewhat critical audience. He spoke with the natural ease of one who was speaking with his friend. His face was rarely beautiful, with both strength and sweetness. The clear sentences, the swift intelligence, the interesting information, the clean-cutting humour all appealed to what Harvard most admired. The picture of the man is vivid; but I can recall only one fragment of the speech. He had been saying how unfair it was to judge all Indians by some conspicuous rascal. "Just think," he said, "how unfair it would be to judge the white man as we often judge the Indian. For instance," he went on, "there was an institution which one year graduated four young men. Within twenty years one of these men had robbed a bank, one had committed murder, another died in a drunken brawl, and the fourth was—myself." (I must confess that my memory fails me just what the crimes were, so I draw on my imagination to that extent; but I am sure that he mentioned three quite lively criminals. And I can still remember how we all jumped with amazement when he reached his climax. Several seconds passed before we gathered ourselves together for the laughter which followed.)

I next saw Bishop Hare at a boys' school, to which he often went because his nephews were pupils there, and also because the boys annually made him a large gift for his Indians. He captivated the boys quite as promptly as the Harvard professors, partly because they instinctively recognized what a fine gentleman he was; and partly because he told in a thrilling way most exciting Indian stories. The way the boys raised their Indian money was to have a paper Indian pinned to the wall in the big school room. A skilful sixth former had made out of paper all manner of Indian belongings from a pony to a feather. This clothing and equipment were sold at auction, piece by piece, to the highest bidder. The room became like the stock exchange in a panic, and the masters kept a watchful eye on the

Photograph by Elmer Chickering.

BISHOP HARE.

little boys, who were apt to bid all their pocket money for the next six months. When a belated master asked what had happened to the school room, a small first former would answer, "Oh, nothin', Sir; we just had Bishop Hare's auction."

A little later I went to live in a diocese next to Bishop Hare's. And there the reverence for him was even greater than in the Eastern College and the Eastern School. This was because he and his work were more intimately known. News came to us that, at the General Convention in Washington in 1898, the whole Church kept his twenty-fifth anniversary as Bishop. We exulted in the story which Bishop Potter told of a dinner in London, when some Englishman asked the Bishop of New York who the very handsome clergyman was across the table. "That," said Bishop Potter, "is the Missionary Bishop of South Dakota." "Oh," said the blasé questioner, "only a missionary bishop." Then Bishop

Potter said there came to him the memory of Thackeray's description of Swift's finding in a desk a lock of Stella's hair, the paper enclosing it being marked with the words, "Only a woman's hair." Then Thackeray makes his comment: "Only a woman's hair; only love, only fidelity, only purity, innocence, beauty; only the tenderest heart in the world."

A good many people were in the habit of saying: "Why should a man like Bishop Hare have been sent to the frontier? Why not some rough and ready person, loud and aggressive? Then Bishop Hare might have been saved for some place capable of appreciating his charm and power." No one would have dared to make such a silly speech to one of Bishop Hare's Indians. Even to look at the picture of a meeting of Bishop Hare's Indian Convocation would convince the most unimaginative of what Bishop Hare meant to the appreciation of the dignified Indian tribesman. A long row of kneeling Indians, out under the open sky, with Bishop Hare kneeling in the middle of the line, tells at one glance what his leadership was. It is one of the fallacies of the academic mind that anybody will do for leadership on the frontier. There is something about the open-air life, accustomed to broad stretches of sky and the clean earth, which appreciates, as the man of the city cannot appreciate, all the niceties and carefulness of the gentleman. When I lived in Minnesota, the frontier had moved far to the westward, but I knew in my congregation men who remembered the days of the pioneer. One of the details most often recalled of the pioneer missionary was that when he walked several miles to officiate in a mission chapel, he never entered the chancel in the shoes in which he had made the dusty journey. He kept in the robing-room a pair of clean shoes which he put on for the service. My friends even remembered that they were "patent leather"! Part of their love for him

was contained in this nice appreciation of
what was fitting in "the courts of the Lord's
House." If one has rough and noisy people
to place, let them be put in the great centre
where there are people of all sorts to satisfy.
The frontier must have the gentleman always, and he will be loved for many reasons,
one of them being because he *is* a gentleman.

It was often asked how a man of Bishop
Hare's apparently delicate physique and
sensibilities could survive Indian hospitality
on his long missionary journeys through the
Indian country. That was a difficulty
which he frankly faced, and his common
sense and his courtesy solved it without destroying his digestion or hurting the feel-
ings of his Indian flock. After due and
satisfactory explanation he travelled about
with a tent and a cook, and the whole
"Episcopal Palace" went wherever the
Bishop went. Doubtless he lived longer as
Bishop of South Dakota than he would

have lived in any other diocese of the Church. He neither expected nor desired any pity for visitations which made him only the more rugged and brought him to people who gave him trust and love nowhere to be excelled.

Because I lived in a town where there was a theological school and therefore knew a good many younger clergy or those about to enter the Ministry, he would often ask me questions about men. I received a telegram one day asking if I would be at home that evening, and if he might drop in upon me. I tried to persuade him really to break his long journey, and to stay with me for at least the night. But he said that it was impossible, for he must be at home; so he stayed only a few hours and caught a midnight train for Sioux Falls. Meantime he plied me with keen and searching questions about men for certain stations which he described. He was alert, and had, I thought, a thorough mastery of every corner of his district: for he was clear about just the sort of man he needed for each place. It was not easy to sleep after I had come home from the station: I kept thinking about an old man who, as a good shepherd, seemed never to relax his watchfulness over the sheep committed to his care.

The next time I saw him after this was at a Missionary Council. There was a covering over one eye. We whispered to one another that the sight of the eye was gone and that a most painful disease had set in which could end only in death. But he seemed unconscious of it all. The beauty was not gone; if anything it was intensified by the heroic bearing of suffering. And his word was still with power. It was good to sit beside him and to talk on personal themes; it was even better to sit among the people and to hear him speak to us all, and to feel the devotion which his face and his word aroused. Bishop Whipple was gone:

he was now the Grand Old Man of our wide
Northwest. He could not help knowing
the affectionate loyalty of the whole Church.

Not long after this I became the rector
of an Eastern parish. I was one morning
called to the telephone. The voice said, to
my amazement: "I am Bishop Hare; I am
at Bishop Vinton's. Could you possibly
come up to see me?" Of course I said Yes;
I dropped everything, delighted at the
thought of seeing him once more; and
started at once. I found him quite the same
cheerful, self-forgetting person as of old,
but the wound on the face was larger. I
knew that there could not be many months
more of suffering. After a few personal
words, he began briskly: "I want your advice about three men, all of whom you know.
I have high-sounding letters from bishops
recommending them—but I don't care anything about bishops' recommendations."
Bishop Vinton, well endowed with humour,
coughed a dry little cough, and said, "Bishop

Hare, wouldn't you rather I went out?" "Oh, no," said Bishop Hare laughing; "I don't mind you: you can stay." Then he turned to me, saying, "Now I am going to describe these three men, one by one, just as they appear to me; and I want you to tell me if I am right." He took up one; described his personal habits, his abilities, his limitations. It was all so picturesque as well as accurate that I laughed in spite of myself. "Then you agree to that?" he asked. "Yes," I said, "to the last syllable." So he took up the second and the third; and when he was done, it was as if he had read my own mind. I could only confirm his estimates. Just then the telephone bell rang, and Bishop Vinton, who answered it, reported that it was the Rev. Mr. Faithope of Providence, who wished to speak to Bishop Hare. When Bishop Hare had disappeared into the hall to answer the message, Bishop Vinton smiled and said with a twitch at his beard, "Do you know any gos-

sip about Mr. Faithope of Providence?"
Then Bishop Vinton added, "Faithope told
me just now on the telephone that he was
free to move, though the relations between
him and his parish were of the pleasantest,
and there was no reason why he should
move. . . . Ever hear anything like that
before?" And so in a few minutes I de-
parted, leaving two gay and happy bishops.

I never saw Bishop Hare again, and I
was glad that I saw him last in the sunlight.
I forgot the shadow that was hanging over
him; and I suspect that to him it was no
shadow. It was only the beckoning towards
the brighter day.

Just after Bishop Hare's death, I became
rector of still another parish. A neighbour
told me that some of Bishop Hare's Indians
were in the Wild West Show, which was
being played not many blocks from my
church. My neighbour said that these Indians were eager to receive the Holy Communion. Could I by any chance provide the

service for them? Grateful for the chance of serving Bishop Hare's Indians in any way, I asked him to say how gladly I should provide the service at any hour convenient for them. A day and an hour were fixed. Our organist and choristers shared in the service. One small boy, in the infirmary, informed the matron, "I just have to get up, and go to that service"—and he went! The time between the morning rehearsal and the afternoon performance of the Wild West Show was so short that the Indians who came to the church were not allowed to remove their paint and feathers. So in all their barbaric splendour they came down the great thoroughfare, and all the city seemed to come with them. They sat in the front pews, and the crowds poured in behind them. The Indians were as unconscious of the crowds as they were of their war-finery. They fixed their eyes on the white-robed choristers and the stately sanctuary. They sang two verses of "Rock of Ages" in Dakota, and then, in due time, they came up with reverent dignity to receive the Holy Communion. I forgot the paint and feathers, even as they forgot them. They were kneeling to receive the strength of Christ for their journey. I knew that they thought of their dear leader, as I was thinking of him; and so thinking, we were all nearer to our Master and his, the Lord Jesus.

WILLIAM REED HUNTINGTON

WILLIAM REED HUNTINGTON

WILLIAM REED HUNTING-TON was one of the most versatile men of his time. He did many things with extraordinary excellence. Glad to be known always as a Christian minister, he brought into his vocation a richness and variety which gave the man of the world a new conception of what it was to be a clergyman. He wrote a good deal of verse; with depth of feeling he united exactness of expression and beauty of phrasing, so deserving the title of poet. He found in the General Convention opportunity to exercise a remarkable skill in lively and brilliant debate. He revived the order of deaconesses, establishing in New York a permanent school for their training. He built up and administered a great institutional parish, meantime yielding profound interest to the construction of a metropolitan cathedral. He was an able preacher, giving to people the concise account of a thorough knowledge and a sensitive experience. He was the friend of other clergymen, a sort of archbishop, consulted by men young and old who felt sure that he would gladly stop his busy life to hear their tale. It made no difference to him whether they lived in a neighbouring street or an island in the Pacific; he was interested in them all—he was their brother in a wide brotherhood of service. With all this variety of work joyfully undertaken, he was first of all a pastor, going from house to house in the parish which was his primary duty, proving himself a tender and loving shepherd of individual souls.

Early in my life I came to know this man by reputation. Then I chanced to sit in this congregation or that convention as the power of his personality smote across its life. At length I came to know him, and I think he counted me a friend. I certainly looked up to him as one of my masters.

I saw him first in a college chapel, to which he had come to preach a Sunday evening sermon. I remember the clearness and crispness of the faultless English; I remember that I had a student's respect for the well-ordered and dignified presentation of a solid argument; but I was not impressed, as I was later impressed, by the man's fire. I heard him afterwards in the General Convention and in Church Congresses; I believe I never heard him preach again, so that I cannot properly speak of his qualities as a preacher; but I have the impression that he did not let himself go in a sermon as he freed himself in less formal utterances. It may have been part of his Puritan inheritance that he exercised restraint and reserve in a sermon, as fitting reverence towards the house of God. But, more than that, his parishioners for twenty-one years at All Saints', Worcester, and for twenty-six years at Grace Church, New York, would say that it was because he weighed his words and scrupulously taught exactly what he had proved in his own life. That is why his preaching sank deep into their hearts: life and words went together. When he was dying he dictated the message, "Have my people told that I die in the faith which I have preached to them, and that it has brought me peace at the last." They understood.

I next heard him speak at a School Prize Day. He was amusing and delightful, not by telling any story or anecdote, but by a whimsical humour which held the youngest boy as it held the oldest parent. He said that at a recent dinner party an alumnus of the school had warned him not to spend his speech in praising the headmaster—the boys were very tired of hearing the prize day orator pour out the praise. "So," said Dr.

Huntington, "though I have the highest regard for your headmaster, though I know
his genius as a guide of youth, though I
value his personal friendship for us all, yet
ten thousand horses all pulling together
could not drag this opinion out of me."
Afterwards I had a chance to talk with him
alone. We had both been reading Bishop
Clark's *Reminiscences,* and I said how odd
it seemed to be reading these gay and witty
papers in the pages of a staid theological
magazine. "Yes," he answered instantly,
"it's like opening a bottle of champagne in
a hearse."

Years passed. I read his speeches, his
articles, his books; but I did not see him;
for my work was far from New York. One
Winter, however, when I was spending a
week in New York, I found myself a fellow-
guest at the dinner table of a friend whom
we happened to have in common. Before
the dinner we chanced to be thrown together,
and I forgot that anyone else was in the

room. I seemed to know a new Dr. Huntington, whom I had never known before. I found him taking hold of my life, giving himself to me—a younger workman in his craft—as if I were his equal, thus assuming that our friendship had begun. It is one of the thrilling moments of which one cannot say much, when one is conscious of winning a noble friend of whose interest one is henceforth perpetually sure. When at the table I found my seat next to his, I was able to speak out to him, as he continued to speak out to me. After that he would send me anything he published, and I sent him anything of mine which found its way to print. He never received these tokens in silence, but quickly sent his estimate of sermon or of book; so that I came to think as I let a manuscript go to the printer, "Is this the sort of thing I should want Dr. Huntington to read?" His criticism always brought me help and joy.

I think the most brilliant words I ever

Photograph by Henry Havelock Pierce, New York and Boston.

WILLIAM REED HUNTINGTON.

heard from him were spoken at the Church
Congress in Pittsburgh, in a discussion on
The Name of the Church. He frankly admitted that the name, The Protestant Episcopal Church, was not a good name, but it
was as good as we deserved. It was in any
case no worse than the name of our nation,
The United States of America. Indeed the
only perfect names were the names which
chemists gave their compounds. Ferrous
Sulphate, for example, fitted like a glove.
The only difficulty was that such exact
names could be applied only to things which
were dead. Living things grew up to names
which they then received. Richard the Lion
Heart, Charles the Bold, and Peter the
Great were not so named at the font. He
could not believe that we could gather people into our pavilion by adopting some am-
bitious name. Neither could he think it a
dignified position in which to be found, this
frequent sitting on the Pope's doorstep
waiting vainly for the bell to be answered.

We must be greater in mind, body, and soul —then the name would take care of itself.

People sometimes felt that he did not care much for the younger element in life. After this Church Congress I wrote him that I had tried to get at him to thank him for the inspiration of his paper, but, I said, I had found him so thronged by older men that I couldn't get at him. By the next post came his answer: "I wish you hadn't given up. I don't care anything about these older men. It's the younger men I want to see— the men who have the future."

In this connection I recall that one of his parishioners once told me how much he had awed her as a girl. Then one day she felt that she must get his help. She went to the rectory, waiting for her turn to go down the little staircase into his study. She was "all of a tremble" as she went into the shadows of the Gothic room. He seemed very businesslike as she began her story. She had come to ask him if he wouldn't see that a

certain young man (whom she named)
should be confirmed. With a flash of his
eye, he turned upon her, suddenly asking,
"You're engaged?" "No," she said, "we
wish we were." "Why aren't you, then?"
he said with a staccato accent. "My mother
says I'm too young." "Not a bit of it," he
replied earnestly: "I'll see your mother."
This was most comforting, and it was never
again to be difficult to come to the rectory
for advice. "And about the confirmation?"
she asked. For the first time in the inter-
view he smiled, and he said very gently,
"Don't you really think the young man had
better come to see me himself?"

In later years I never came to New York
without going to see him. I did try not
to stay long, but he did not know my pious
intention of brevity, and I always marvelled
that he could settle down in the middle of
his day for a leisurely talk as if he had nothing else to do. It was part of his genius.
Once as I was departing he asked me where

I was going. When I said that I was going far uptown, he said that he too was off in the same direction: he had a motor at the door—wouldn't I go with him? As soon as the motor door had clicked behind us and we were comfortably rolling up the street he became confidential. I spoke of a very famous person whom practically everyone praised. "I never liked him," he confessed —and then he told me why! We passed from person to person, from topic to topic. He spoke of a man who ten years before had been, as everyone thought, utterly commonplace; who now had so grown as to be, he thought, really a notable leader. He spoke of college, of the Church, of a man's loyalties. Then suddenly the motor stopped before a palace. His face was inexpressibly changed. "You wouldn't think," he said, "that grief could get into a house like that —but it's there—most terrible grief."

I suppose that Dr. Huntington's public service was most clearly shown in sessions

of the General Convention. When the
Prayer Book was spoken of as "our incom-
parable liturgy," he persuaded the Church
to revise it; he originated the famous terms
of the Chicago-Lambeth Quadrilateral; his
was the wisest and most constant voice for
Christian Unity. I may give only one instance of his power in debate which I wit-
nessed in the Richmond Convention of 1907,
his last General Convention. Someone had
proposed that the Church consecrate three
Negro bishops, and then bid the Southern
Negroes set up housekeeping for themselves
in an independent Church. The Northern
delegates evidently felt that here was a
question to be settled by the South. One
Southerner after another spoke against the
plan. Very appealing were the references
to the Negro "mammies," loved almost as
mothers: "We can't set these people adrift,"
was the conclusion; "they belong to us; they
need us." We were all much moved, and
there seemed nothing more which could be

said. To everyone's surprise, in the strange stillness which had taken hold of the Convention, Dr. Huntington rose. "We have heard," he began, "that the Negro needs the white man. I want to say that the white man needs the Negro: we need his gentle voice; we need his affectionate heart; we need his loyalty unto death." The silence was intenser still. After all, the North had said the last word in a great debate.

When he died he was one of the conspicuous men of New York; yet he had never striven nor cried, his name was seldom in the papers, he never sought attention. It was the thoroughness of his workmanship which told. To this thoroughness was added another quality which is a gift from God: he did the ordinary things of life in a new way, so that one felt that distinction had been conferred upon the commonplace, and all life was illumined. His "Thank you" and "I am sorry" were never conventional: he someway always brought the ever new

richness of his kindness and sympathy into
them. The most apt illustration of this
trait which I can recall is the way he took
to show the sorrow of Grace Church with
the Hebrew race for a dreadful tragedy
which had befallen the Jews in Russia. The
Hebrews of New York had organized a
mournful procession which marched up
Broadway, that the world might know how
much they cared. All the time that the long
procession was passing, the bell of Grace
Church was tolled, and the Rector, now an
old man, stood with bared head before the
door. The Jews who walked past Grace
Church on that bleak day will never forget
the tenderness of that tribute to human
brotherhood. An illustration of this trait
in words many will recall is his dedication
to Bishop Huntington, his old Rector,
under whom he began his ministry (it was
inscribed in the last volume of sermons
which he published): "To the memory of
Frederic Dan Huntington, Bishop, Doctor

in Divinity, Doctor of Letters and of Laws,
Father in God to many souls and to mine."
The very simplicity of it is startling.

When all is recorded of Dr. Huntington's public service as a citizen and as a
Churchman, I suspect that those who knew
him would claim for his private conversation and companionship the highest mani-
festation of his work in the world. That is
because he was pre-eminently a Christian
pastor. Through a strange turn of events
I was to know intimately many of those who
knew him best. Through them I came to
open a new chapter in my friendship with
Dr. Huntington, for I was to find him,
though seemingly dead to this world, altogether alive in the hearts of his friends.
And there I have learned the depth of his
sincerity, the perseverance of his watchful
care, the blaze of his righteous scorn, the
patience of his hope, his unforgetting love.
I was sitting one night with one of his
parishioners and friends, when I spoke my

reverence for his former rector: the light kindled in the eyes of my friend, as he said simply, "Huntington saw the right—and he did it—always."